Emotional Literacy

Assessment and Intervention

AGES 11 to 16

Published by nferNelson Publishing Company Ltd
The Chiswick Centre
414 Chiswick High Road
LONDON W4 5TF, UK

Tel: ++44 (0) 208 996 8444
www.nfer-nelson.co.uk

nferNelson is a division of Granada Learning Limited, part of Granada plc

Emotional Literacy: Assessment and Intervention – Ages 11 to 16
Code 0090008696   ISBN 0-7087-0364-X 1(11.03)

Designed by Oxford Designers & Illustrators

Printed by Ashford Colour Press, Gosport, Hampshire

Emotional Literacy

Assessment and Intervention

Southampton Psychology Service
Editor: Adrian Faupel

USER'S GUIDE

At-a-glance guide to using *Emotional Literacy: Assessment and Intervention – Ages 11 to 16*

This Guide contains everything you need to evaluate the emotional literacy of an individual or group of students and then to design an intervention, based on the results of the assessment, to support students in developing their emotional literacy. You may find it helpful to follow the steps below.

1. It will be useful to first familiarise yourself with the materials by reading the **Foreword** by Peter Sharp and the rationale for assessing emotional literacy in **Chapters 1 to 4** written by Adrian Faupel.

2. Use the photocopiable **Emotional Literacy Checklists** on pages 125 to 129 to assess emotional literacy. Instructions for administration and scoring are given in Chapter 5, page 25. There are three optional checklists, for completion by the student, teacher and parent, all of which have been standardised. Use the information on pages 16 and 25 to help you decide which suits your purpose – they can be used singly or in combination. From the responses to the checklists you will be able to obtain an overall emotional literacy score for the individual. If you use the Teacher and/or Parent Checklist you will also be able to compare different perceptions of the student plus obtain five subscale scores that look at the main components of emotional literacy as defined in this Guide and by Goleman (1996):

    - self-awareness
    - self-regulation
    - motivation
    - empathy
    - social skills.

    If wished, the scores can all be transferred to the photocopiable **Student Score Sheet** on page 130 for ease of reference.

3. Use the transparent **scoring keys** on pages 131 to 133 to ensure easy and accurate scoring of the responses to the checklists.

4. Using the results of the checklists, you can then plan appropriate support for the individual or group by selecting **interventions** from pages 45 to 100. You can 'mix and match' these activities to suit the needs of the individuals involved and the resources available. Nine steps in the process of teaching emotional literacy are presented on page 24.

5. While carrying out these interventions with your students, you may choose to use the photocopiable **worksheets** from pages 101 to 122. These are clearly numbered and referred to in the text, for example **Worksheet 1**.

6. You can re-test with the **checklists** to monitor both the progress of students and the effectiveness of your intervention.

Contents

Foreword

'Poetry is the spontaneous overflow of powerful feelings:
it takes its origin from emotion recollected in tranquillity.'
William Wordsworth, 1770–1850

There is an increasing recognition in education, and indeed beyond that into business and commerce, that the affective domain has been seriously overlooked. All the indicators are that emotional literacy is a significant contributor to success as measured on a whole range of criteria.

The publication of this important and valuable set of materials, *Emotional Literacy: Assessment and Intervention – Ages 11 to 16* (and its sister publication for younger pupils), comes at a time of rapid development in the emotional literacy agenda, and happily coincides with the publication by the Department for Education and Skills of advice and guidance to schools about social, emotional and behavioural skills (SEBS).

Promoting emotional literacy is a relatively unused potential lever in raising and promoting the national standards agenda at primary and secondary phases. By building upon and reinforcing current teaching and learning strategies and approaches and by providing a focus on the affective domain, this Guide can really add value to the work of teachers, learning support assistants (LSAs) and support services and can act as a powerful additional dimension to raising standards, improving behaviour and increasing attendance in a sustainable and humane way. When used well these materials will also help educators make a valuable contribution to recent and related debates and findings on young people's mental health. Assessment and intervention can help to increase young people's resilience to the stresses of targets and competition and help to inoculate against increasing trends in mental health problems.

Southampton was the first city in the world to adopt a city-wide strategy to promote emotional literacy in and beyond education, which has been developing now for over five years. Emotional literacy in Southampton remains one of the top three priorities within their strategic education plan. Those who compiled this Guide have 'walked the talk' by working successfully at all levels of this exciting and fulfilling agenda, specifically:

- *intrapersonal level* (the 'I'/'me' level) – the authors have measured, scrutinised and developed their own emotional literacy through a systematic and enduring process embedded in the learning culture of Southampton City Council;
- *interpersonal level* (the 'you and me' or 'me and others' level) – the authors worked on a programme of developing emotional literacy for themselves, young people, parents, LEA officers, headteachers, teachers, LSAs, governors and other education stakeholders;
- *suprapersonal level* (the organisational or systemic level) – for Southampton this meant the team, the LEA and, later, the city council.

This brilliant piece of work is the culmination of many years' dedication to making a difference for young people, and Adrian Faupel (Editor) and his colleagues have crafted an invaluable resource. This resource should become essential reading in the toolkit of all educators and, in particular, for headteachers and senior teachers who have a leadership and management role. It will become an indispensable manual for SENCOs, PSHE, Citizenship, and Healthy Schools co-ordinators and all those working to promote emotional literacy.

Emotional Literacy: Assessment and Intervention exists to inform purposeful and well-intentioned assessment that leads to support, encouragement and, where appropriate, challenge or intervention to enhance the social and emotional development and well-being of young people.

Congratulations to Adrian and his colleagues for all their efforts, and to nferNelson for commissioning this work.

Peter Sharp
BSc PGCE DipEd CertEdPsych MA CPsychol
Principal Consultant, Mouchel plc
peter.sharp@mouchel.com

Acknowledgements

Members of the Southampton Psychology Service (2002–03):

Elizabeth Herrick — Principal Educational Psychologist

Jo Corcoran
Julie Goodman
Julia Katherine
Karen Morris
— Senior Educational Psychologists

Sheila Burton *(to July 2002)*
Caroline Carpenter
Diana Holmes
Kerry Jackson
Plaxy Matthews
Alyce McCourt
Fiona Powell
Caitríona Scully
Gillian Shotton *(to July 2002)*
Colin Woodcock
— Educational Psychologists

Karen Davies
Helen Harman
— Family Inclusion Support Officers

Annie Bigwood
Jill Cook
Debbie Mawdsley
Doreen Pryer
Sarah Weaver
— Emotional Literacy Support Assistants

Jenny Edmonds
Rachael Gass
— Assistant Educational Psychologists *(2001–02)*

Janet Field
Jeanne Gillooly
Janita Hendricks
Jackie Holgate
Isabella Robinson
— Administrative Support Staff

Sincere thanks are due to all the members of the Southampton Psychology Service without whose contribution, in one way or another, *Emotional Literacy: Assessment and Intervention* would never have seen the light of day. As Editor, I have received first-class support from Carole Carlow, Cres Fernandes, Denise Moulton and Louise O'Hara of nferNelson. Their encouragement, cajoling and gentle persistence was very emotionally literate!

Special thanks are also due to the staff, students and parents who first trialled these materials in Southampton – Chamberlayne Park Secondary School, Hightown Primary School, Mansel Junior School, St Denys Primary School and Sinclair Junior School.

Adrian Faupel
Senior Educational Psychologist and Professional & Academic Tutor, University of Southampton

Introduction to the assessment and development of emotional literacy

Emotional Literacy: Assessment and Intervention – Ages 11 to 16 provides practical tools that can be used by anyone involved in the education of children and young people. Their purpose is to discover where students' strengths and weaknesses are in the area of emotional literacy, in order to provide a better understanding of these competences and, where necessary, to highlight areas for intervention. Three standardised checklists enable the user to assess emotional literacy according to the perceptions of:

- adults in school (teachers, learning support assistants, etc.);
- parents and carers at home;
- the young people themselves.

This Guide provides an overview of how to assess and develop emotional literacy. It offers guidelines for teachers, learning support assistants and behaviour support personnel, highlighting why emotional literacy is a crucial topic for schools and focusing on practical rather than theoretical aspects. The Guide describes the main components of emotional literacy, gives guidance about the appropriate uses of the three checklists, and explores how the findings can be used to design interventions for working with students. Finally, suggestions are provided for a range of activities that can be used in a variety of ways as part of a programme to support students in becoming more emotionally literate.

The three checklists form the core of the *Emotional Literacy: Assessment and Intervention – Ages 11 to 16* materials. Singly or, preferably, in combination, they enable the user to identify aspects of emotional literacy needing attention.

- They can act as a baseline measure for year groups or whole classes of students prior to some focused curriculum work or other intervention, and then as a means of measuring progress afterwards.
- They can be used with individual students – the school and parental views provide a richness of comparison about how the student is perceived at school and in the home, and lead to a mutual understanding between home and school to inform intervention.
- They can form the basis of individual counselling, helping the students to become more self-aware by providing feedback both from adults in the school and from their parents. Students can compare these other views with their own judgements about themselves and how they think, feel and behave. When used in this interactive way during individual counselling sessions, specific items from the checklists may act as a stimulus for ongoing discussion.

The checklists cover five dimensions of emotional literacy:

- self-awareness
- self-regulation (managing one's own emotions)
- motivation
- empathy
- social skills.

It is possible to produce profiles showing areas of strengths and weakness across these dimensions. Although cut-offs derived from the norms of the standardisation sample are given in this Guide, the intention is not to compare children and young people with each other, but rather to pinpoint which areas of emotional literacy in individuals might receive priority for intervention.

The checklists are deliberately short: each takes less than 10 minutes to complete in normal circumstances, when school staff, parents and students are completing them independently. Information on how and when to administer the checklists is given in Chapter 5.

Chapter 1: What is emotional literacy?

A working definition describes emotional literacy as the ability of people to recognise, understand, handle and appropriately express their own emotions and to recognise, understand and respond appropriately to the expressed emotions of others.

The phrase 'emotional literacy' is very recent, although Steiner (1997) first spoke about it some 25 years ago. There are a number of phrases which, to a greater or lesser extent, tap into the general concept – 'social intelligence', 'interpersonal and intra-personal intelligence' and 'emotional intelligence', to name the most common. The concept of 'emotional intelligence' has given rise to heated academic debate, with some querying the appropriateness and meaningfulness of this concept at all, and others describing it as an 'elusive, but appealing, construct'.

We prefer the term 'emotional literacy', not only to avoid some of the negative associations of the word 'intelligence', but also because some aspects of emotional literacy relate to the concept of literacy as we normally use the word. For example, in reading we have to be able to decode the letters and words on the page, using a variety of strategies, in order to read them and extract meaning. In much the same way, the first task of an emotionally literate person is to be able to read or decode signs and symbols – physiological signs within ourselves and also facial expressions, other non-verbal aspects of communication and the general ethos of interpersonal situations. Again, like reading, we create hypotheses as to the meaning of a situation and use a variety of skills to do this. In both reading and emotional literacy, these are largely learned skills that can be directly taught. Such teaching may need to be tailor-made to meet the needs of a particular individual.

Thinking, behaviour and emotion

Traditionally, at least, we think about ourselves and others in terms of the *head* (thinking/cognition), *behaviour* (what we do and the required physical/motor skills), and the *heart* (emotion/feeling). Different schools of psychology have historically emphasised one or the other of these to the relative detriment of the others.

It could be argued that one of the main functions of schools at the height of the Industrial Revolution, when mass education began, was to teach basic skills and to select pupils by ability. Out of this arose the concept of 'intelligence' which appeared to be, for the most part, something fixed and 'given'. Children were selected for schooling on the basis of their 'potential'. IQ testing provoked a dilemma for educationalists: is it meaningful to talk about raising a student's IQ, if indeed it really is something fixed and immutable? It is mainly because of such paradoxes, and because IQ was used simply to compare and divide students into categories, that the term 'emotional literacy' is preferred in this work.

Subsequently, education was dominated by a focus on behaviour. It is clear that appropriate interpersonal behaviours are preconditions for effective learning in classrooms. The skills of classroom management produce that ordered predictable environment necessary for the effective teaching of groups of students. Good classroom management techniques are designed to achieve this, with many of these techniques clearly based upon behavioural theories of learning.

Political and parental pressures, over the last 20 or 30 years, have led to academic attainments and behavioural aspects of education becoming increasingly dominant. Schools are weighed, measured and often found wanting on measures of academic attainment and on attendance rates and exclusion behaviour. What has been largely neglected has been any focus on the third aspect of human functioning – that of the emotions.

Of course, good schools and good teachers have always been concerned about 'the whole person' and, over the years, psychologists such as Freud, Adler and Bowlby have recognised the importance of emotions and feelings. Although it may be difficult to tie down precisely what emotional literacy is, its major contribution is that it redirects the attention of educators and parents to the affective, emotional side of human functioning. This is, some would argue, the primary purpose of education over and above issues of academic attainments and behaviour management. Emotional literacy aims to reintroduce that sense of 'the whole person' that has been overlooked by an emphasis on attainment.

Although emotional literacy is a rather abstract and 'woolly' concept, which is quite difficult to define and tie down empirically, the concept nevertheless does capture a shift in emphasis following many years of an almost exclusive focus on cognition and behaviour in education. The understanding and management of emotions are increasingly being seen as central to the whole process of growth and development into adulthood and there are now serious question marks over the usefulness of academic attainments and qualifications if the foundations of interpersonal and community-building skills and competences are absent.

Emotional literacy has aspects of both thinking and behaviour. The recognition and understanding of our own and other people's emotions appears to be more highly related to cognitive 'intelligence', whereas the ability to handle and appropriately express emotions is more concerned with behaviour. Emotional literacy is concerned with *myself and my emotions* on the one hand and with *other people and their emotions* on the other. It is about keeping in control and maintaining high levels of performance when *my own emotions* are threatening to take over, and also about managing stress or conflict in the face of *other people's emotions*.

Emotional literacy and the individual

Research and experience both testify that the quality of our relationships has a real impact on overall happiness and fulfilment. Positive relationships appear essential both to the overall quality of our lives and the ability to cope with inevitable losses, frustrations, disappointments and failures. There is increasing evidence that how we feel is especially important in influencing what we do. How we feel also influences how we think, though it is probably even more true to say that how we think about ourselves, other people and the world around us affects how we feel. Feeling, thinking and behaviour each interact with each other, and emotions have a core role to play in how we function as human beings. There are obvious overlaps with the notion of self-esteem, self-worth, etc.

Self-esteem

How we think about ourselves clearly influences how we get on with other people. Emotional literacy has, therefore, very close links with the quality of peer relationships. How we get on with our peers from about the age of three or four onwards seems to be of crucial significance for our later adjustment into adolescence and then later still as adults. So, there are also aspects of emotional literacy that overlap with social skills and interpersonal competences and with mental health (for instance, the 'Healthy Schools' initiative, DfES, 1998).

Inclusion

The relationship between low levels of emotional literacy and the inability to handle relationships is strongly related to poor behaviour[1] and under-achievement in schools and also to how many, and which, students are excluded. It is not without significance that emotional literacy work in schools is often prompted by interventions (for example, anger management groups) designed for those students at risk of permanent exclusion. Most permanent and serious exclusions are the result of poor behaviour that is highly emotional in origin and tone. The best and worst of our behaviour is usually very emotional! Emotional literacy is, therefore, strongly related to the more general issue of social inclusion.

Academic attainment and self-worth

The link between emotional literacy and academic attainment is less clear-cut, at least as regards the empirical evidence. Does feeling good equal learning well? Probably, on balance, it does, but we may have to unpack what 'learning well' really means. If it means simply passing exams, we have a problem in that the most emotionally illiterate of students may achieve very highly. This may be due to a neurotic need to be best and the use of academic brilliance as a refuge from the more threatening demands of relationships. Achieving academic accolades certainly does not equate to high levels of emotional literacy. What seems more likely is that the ability to give up immediate short-term and emotional needs for the sake of longer-term benefits relates to success in academic learning. 'Motivation' is one of the key dimensions of emotional literacy.

Problem-solving and creativity, as opposed to superficial rote learning, are probably the kinds of learning really needed today. It would appear that the former might relate to high levels of emotional literacy, as such learning involves an openness to the unpredictable and to risk. It demands high levels of emotional security and a belief in one's own inherent worth. Such personal beliefs are related to qualities of attachment and are a prerequisite for genuine self-awareness, empathy and motivation. For the individual student, therefore, emotional literacy appears to be central to both interpersonal and academic functioning and at the heart of feelings of self-worth and dignity.

[1] *Please note that the phrases 'poor behaviour', 'bad behaviour' and 'good behaviour' are used in order to be succinct when repeatedly referring to behaviours that are more fully described elsewhere in the Guide, although we recognise that these are value judgements.*

Emotional literacy in classrooms and schools

Emotional literacy cannot just be discussed in relation to the individual. It is important to be wary of a within-person deficit model of emotional literacy. It is equally important to remember that our emotionally literate behaviour is profoundly influenced by the context or environment in which we function. In practical terms, it is not possible and there is little value in trying to apportion the contribution of within-person and environmental factors in the development and maintenance of emotional literacy. What we do know is that, except in extremely rare circumstances, behaviour is a function of the reciprocal interaction of the individual and his or her environment. Each individual, with a unique genetic make-up, a unique family history and ongoing experience, both *influences* and *is influenced by* the immediate context in which they find themselves. While this is true of academic learning as well, it is particularly true of emotional literacy which is essentially about the handling of our emotions in relationships with others. Therefore, there is an inherent social and interpersonal dimension to emotional literacy.

The emotional literacy of the peer group, of teachers and of learning support assistants are all important contributions to the emotional development of the individual student. So, it is meaningful to think in terms of emotional literacy of classrooms, schools and even LEAs. The development of the checklists that assess the competences and skills of individual students should not be interpreted as an endorsement of a pathologising within-person model. In fact, although emotional literacy interventions are often geared to students at risk, we believe that emotional literacy is for all students and particularly endorse interventions that are based on an emotional literacy curriculum for all. These might include, for example, PSHE initiatives such as *Circle Time* (Mosely & Tew, 1999), *PATHS* (Greenberg *et al.*, 1995), *Second Step* (Committee for Children, 1999) and some parts of the *Citizenship Curriculum* (QCA, 2002).

Emotional literacy and society

Emotions ignore thinking about longer-term consequences. If we have the ability to manage our own emotions, it means that we do not respond simply to current pressures at the expense of what we rationally know to be in our own and others' best interests.

Thinking about consequences falls within the domain of reason and rationality. In contrast, most of our anti-social destructive behaviour stems from the negative emotions of anxiety, anger and depression. These emotions are essentially responses to perceived threat, and particularly threats to our self-esteem, our value and our lovableness – to our sense of belonging. Our emotionally illiterate behaviour threatens the sense of self-esteem and worthwhileness of others – in some way it demeans them ('denying meaning'). Similarly, the emotionally illiterate behaviour of other people is precisely the behaviour that demeans 'me'. It is here that emotional literacy has overlaps with Citizenship Education and with Moral Education.

● Emotional literacy as a primary aim of schooling

Emotional literacy should not be seen as a fringe activity for schools, since it is at the heart of what schools are all about. The core activity of education is the building of community. Community is about how individuals develop and maintain their own sense of value and self-esteem while at the same time maintaining that of others.

These issues challenge us to respond to longer-term aims and goals rather than to the immediate here and now. Academic brilliance and high attainments in national tests, GCSEs and A-levels can pale into insignificance when we fail to develop genuine community. It should be remembered that emotional literacy is just as important for the successful students as for those who feel they do not belong and are disaffected. The consequences of people feeling that they do not belong are being played out in our towns and in the classrooms and grounds of our schools and colleges.

Chapter 2: The dimensions of emotional literacy

Different authors have come up with a variety of components that they believe make up emotional literacy. Most of these are long and detailed lists of skills and competences and are usually related to the adult world of work. Many of these skills and competences are not really applicable to children and adolescents and, so far, there has been little direct work with children and young people.

Although a number of instruments have been developed for use with adults (for example, *Emotional Intelligence Questionnaire* by Dulewicz & Higgs, 1999; *Bar-On Emotional Quotient Inventory* by Bar-On, 1997; *EQ Map* by Cooper & Sawaf, 1995), particularly in the area of selection for promotion at work, even that is a relatively new area and is continually subject to revision and re-interpretation. Not a great deal of work has so far been carried out on the assessment of the emotional literacy of children and young people.

For these materials we have adapted Goleman's (1996) fairly broad classification of the knowledge, skills and competences that contribute to emotional literacy as these appear to be relevant to the emotional and social development of children and young people. In his pioneering work, Goleman distinguishes between personal competence (which is about how we manage ourselves) and social competence (which concerns how we manage relationships with others). The chart below shows how the areas covered by the checklists in this Guide relate to personal and social competence.

Emotional literacy	
Personal competence	**Social competence**
● Self-awareness	● Empathy
● Self-regulation	● Social skills
● Motivation	

These dimensions are described below. Of course, these can be broken down still further and the boundaries between them are not hard and fast. However, this framework has considerable credence in the literature and is useful for identifying individual student's strengths and areas where further support is needed.

Personal competence

Personal competence consists of three main abilities – self-awareness, self-regulation and motivation.

Self-awareness

Self-awareness is the ability to recognise and understand our own emotions, preferences, strengths and weaknesses. Aristotle saw the first requirement of intelligent human functioning as the ability to 'know thyself', and this is in essence what this first component is about. It is the foundation on which the rest of emotional literacy depends.

Being self-aware involves being emotionally self-aware and having the ability to recognise our own emotions. To this end, we need to be able to discriminate between our various emotions and, in turn, this means that we have to be able to name or label these emotions. The ability to categorise is intimately linked with the development of appropriate language skills. Recognition is, however, not enough: we need to also understand our emotions in the sense that we appreciate how emotions can affect what we think, say and do.

Self-awareness also requires accurate self-assessment. This means knowing our strengths and weaknesses, what is within our own competence and what is beyond us. Grossly inflated views of our abilities are as dangerous to emotional health as continually putting ourselves down. Self-awareness is about realistic and balanced views of attainments and competences. In addition to a realistic assessment of our skills and competences, there is also the need to value ourselves as a person and to be able to distinguish between the belief in our inherent value and lovableness on the one hand and the skills and competences we possess on the other.

Self-regulation

Emotions are clearly a major force in driving what we think, say and do. Of themselves they are fundamentally good and useful, but they can be a force for either good or evil. The primary purpose of emotions is to enable us to survive and flourish both physically and psychologically in what is potentially a threatening and hostile world. Emotions relate to the parts of our brain that were among the first to develop, particularly in relation to instinctual responses to threat (individual survival) and reproduction (survival of the species). There is a very powerful physiological basis to our emotions and, because these involve physiological preparations for strenuous and sometimes violent exertion (particularly the fight and flight responses to threat), they are usually described in terms of physiological 'arousal'.

We are not, however, simply animals governed by instinctual arousal in response to threat. We have highly developed information-processing and logical problem-solving abilities. The relationship between our thinking (rational) and emotional (physiological) selves is a complex one, with the potential for emotions to work with the rational reasonable part of us or against it. Emotions are really concerned only with immediate issues. Reason is generally concerned with longer-term considerations, weighing up the pros and cons, not simply for the immediate present but for the quite distant future as well.

So there is a potential for real conflict between the requests of reason and the demands of emotions. Goleman describes this potential conflict in terms of 'emotional hijacking' with emotions taking over or boiling over (Goleman, 1996, p.13). When this happens, anger or panic can make us do things that we later regret because they have all manner of unpleasant longer-term consequences. For physiological reasons, at moments of intense emotion the senses become heightened and very alert but the mind becomes dull and incapable of rational and clear thinking. The greater and more intense the levels of arousal, the less able are we to problem solve and think rationally.

It now becomes obvious that an emotionally literate person must have the ability to master these powerful impulses and to control the urge to act simply for the here and now – this is what we mean by handling or self-regulating our emotions. It is not about denying them, seeing them as bad, or even ignoring them, but about learning how to use our emotions for our own and others' longer-term good. The emotionally literate person does not stifle and suppress true feelings, but understands his or her emotions and uses them to fulfil longer-term personal and/or interpersonal needs.

Emotionally literate people are, therefore, good at handling stress. Stress is simply another word for a perceived dangerous threat to our physical or psychological survival. People who are good at managing stress have learned to develop strategies that mean they do not have to give vent to violent and impulsive emotions. They use *assertive* responses which avoid the two pitfalls stress can drive us into – excessive aggression (fight) and undue submission or withdrawal (flight). Coping with stress is about being emotionally resilient, bouncing back after knock-backs, controlling our tempers, facing our feelings and resolving conflict by using constructive and non-violent processes. Emotions have not only to be managed or handled, they have to be expressed appropriately. Appropriateness, in this context, means using those strategies that strengthen our own sense of value and worth and build up a sense of worth of others.

Motivation

We are all aware of very gifted individual students who sometimes spectacularly fail to fulfil their potential in school and others who, with limited resources, achieve extraordinarily well. It is motivation that appears to be the key. Indeed, there are some who maintain that it is the crucial variable in raising standards of individuals and groups. Motivation is essentially linked with emotion and they both share the same root etymologically: motivation is about what 'moves us', what 'grabs us'. To appreciate how emotionally literate students are also highly motivated, it is necessary to do some unpacking of the concept of motivation.

Motivation has to do with two questions:

- Why do people choose to do one thing out of an almost limitless number of options?
- Why do some people persist with a particular option, while others give up at the first signs of difficulty or hindrance?

So motivation is about both our choice of goals and our determination to reach these goals. Emotionally literate students are those who have worked out where they want to get to. This means that they have clearly understood where their own long-term interests lie, but in the context of living with other people. The opposite of this, the emotionally illiterate student, has no clearly formulated long-term goals but drifts aimlessly in response to the emotional pushes and pulls of the moment. All the significant outcomes of education demand that we put longer-term goals before short-term ones. The typically 'disaffected' student is one whose 'affect' (that is, emotion) is directed towards goals other than educational ones. They have no affection or warmth for the things they are asked to do in schools and frequently, too, no affection for those people who try to educate them. So, at the very least, unmotivated students have different goals from those of their educators. The behaviour frequently exhibited by such students is an expression of this rejection of the goals and values of schooling.

Furthermore, it is very difficult for people whose emotions are uncontrolled to have the necessary focus and attention required for learning – they have high levels of arousal but these are diffuse and do not allow the person to sustain attention and focus. Emotionally literate students, on the other hand, are good learners as they can be physiologically very alert but, at the same time, are clear thinking and focused on what needs to be done and able to problem solve how to do it: they can think and act efficiently and purposefully.

There is currently considerable debate as to the nature of learning required of students at the beginning of the 21st century. Without venturing into that debate, it is clear that the most successfully 'rounded' students are those who enjoy what they are learning. They are intrinsically motivated. The distinction between intrinsic motivation (which certainly involves emotions of pleasure and enjoyment) and extrinsic motivation (where we do things because of external incentives) is not as clear-cut as it has sometimes been portrayed. Some forms of extrinsic motivation involve a considerable degree of personal commitment – and commitment has emotional overtones. There are two kinds of committed students – those motivated by the hope of success and those motivated by the fear of failure. Those motivated by success are likely to be more emotionally literate.

Dweck's work (1999) provides a fascinating examination of this whole topic. Her research has clearly demonstrated that children can acquire two fundamentally different views of themselves in relation to learning. One view, the 'entity' theory, leads to the belief that ability is 'fixed' ('*I am clever*'). When faced with difficult tasks, the prime motive for individuals who hold this view is to protect their self-esteem against any challenge that might undermine the belief. One strategy to protect this belief is to give up without trying ('*If I haven't tried, I haven't failed*'). The alternative view, the 'incremental' theory, sees ability as open to development with effort and practice. When these individuals are presented with a difficult task, they view this as a challenge to be overcome and tend to put more effort into the task rather than giving up. The way children are praised in their formative years seems to be crucially important in influencing which fundamental schema about their ability they adopt. Praise for effort appears more likely to lead to an incremental rather than an entity view: the entity view is encouraged when inherent qualities are praised ('*You are very clever*').

Finally, in the area of motivation, another aspect of contemporary schooling has emotional implications – co-operative learning. Students are unable to co-operate unless they have a degree of commitment to shared goals, when the goals of other people mesh to some extent with their own. There is a clear link between the personal skills and competences of understanding, managing and expressing our own emotions with the other main aspect of emotional literacy – namely, how we understand and manage the emotions of other people.

Social competence

This consists of two main abilities – empathy and social skills.

Empathy

Emotionally literate people certainly need to understand and manage their own emotions, but this is nearly always in the context of being with other people. The way we understand the people around us, and why they do what they do, will profoundly affect the quality of our relationships and the kinds of emotional stresses we are going to experience. So the first task of these vital people-skills is to be able to notice, read and be sensitive to what other people are feeling and thinking. This cannot be achieved without attention and listening skills. If we do not notice how other people are feeling, we cannot begin to understand and then handle the emotional messages they give to us. Thus, the foundation of empathy is listening and being attentive to the messages that others are sending us.

What are we listening to? Of course the words shared are important but, in the area of interpersonal relationships, it appears that we communicate much more through non-verbal channels. Emotionally literate people are able to read the messages about feelings that others are communicating through facial expression, for example, and can identify what the other person is likely to be feeling. There are a variety of other ways in which people communicate their perceptions, their understandings and emotional reactions to what is going on. These include all the slight variations in eye contact, intensity of gaze, tone, pitch and volume of the voice, body posture, subtle body movements and rates of breathing. We need to be able to pick up the cues from this vast array of subtle pieces of information and then to work out the meanings and implications for ourselves and for other people.

It is only possible to be sensitive and to understand the perceptions of other people if we have the emotional resources to see the world as the other person sees it. If we are able to do this, based on our understanding of how people feel, we then have the possibility of conveying this understanding by our willingness to help others and to come to their assistance when we see them in distress.

These basic skills lead on to higher levels of emotional literacy where we are not only able to read and interpret facial expressions and body language, but are also able to react and respond to the unspoken needs of others. At the highest level, we also have an understanding of what might be causing the emotions in other people (particularly our part in this). As children grow and mature, they will increasingly develop the subtle skills that enable them to understand the powerful and sometimes difficult emotions of other people directed towards them. This has implications for the skills of conflict resolution and being able to work productively in groups, with the latter including such skills as knowing how to recognise and express to other people their strengths and achievements.

Social skills

Empathy is primarily about understanding how others see the world by listening carefully to all the messages they are giving to us. But the second strand of empathy is our ability to communicate to others that we have indeed listened to them and appreciate that their understandings may be very different from ours. The skills needed are fundamentally concerned with how we influence other people to help them meet our own needs, but in ways that enable others to meet their own needs as well. 'Influence' is used as a catch-all expression for the variety of possible strategies, tactics and behaviours that we can use to achieve this.

There are different levels of social skills. Some of these are discreet skills like using appropriate eye contact, facial expressions, tone and volume of speech, and body posture. Some are rather more general, like the use of humour, smiling, laughter and asking for help when needed. Others are ways of being in a relationship to others, like standing up for ourselves and so on. Human society inevitably brings pressures and conflicts as we are frequently competing with sometimes very demanding people. Other people are going to express to us very strong emotions and an emotionally literate person needs to have the skills to handle these. Conflict resolution and negotiation skills, assertive rather than aggressive or submissive skills, are therefore part of the essential armoury for an emotionally literate person.

Chapter 3: Using the checklists to help raise standards of emotional literacy

Although the academic outcomes of education are important, previous chapters have discussed how other aspects of student development are equally important. Emotional literacy can be considered as the essential foundation of an inclusive and democratic society. How can the emotional literacy checklists presented in this Guide help schools achieve their aim of raising emotional literacy?

Monitoring emotional literacy standards

Emotional literacy instruments can play an important role in helping schools to raise standards of emotional literacy. Positive change can be construed as the movement from a current position (where you are now) to a more favourable one (where you want to get to). This puts raising emotional literacy in the context of problem-solving (or solution-finding). A problem has been defined as the gap or discrepancy between the current situation and the necessary or desirable future one. The most reliable, effective and efficient way of solving problems is to do what scientists do – this involves four essential phases in the problem-solving cycle (see Figure 1):

1. Establish precisely where you are now and where you want to get to, collecting data to demonstrate this (this is essentially what we mean by 'assessment').

2. Generate alternative methods of getting there (in scientific jargon these are called 'hypotheses').

3. Implement one of these methods (test the 'hypothesis').

4. Measure whether the gap between 'what is' and 'what should be' has been reduced (evaluation).

Sometimes this process is simplified in terms of a plan, do, review cycle.

Figure 1: The problem-solving cycle

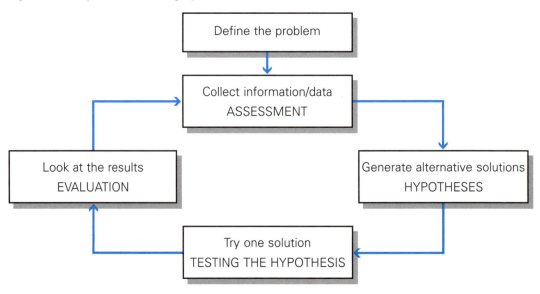

The checklists in this Guide have a vital role to play in the first and fourth phases outlined above. In the first phase of assessment they provide a measure of the current situation (where the students are) and the vision (targets and goals) towards which we hope students will move. They also provide a baseline or benchmark against which progress can be measured. Similarly, in the fourth phase of the problem-solving cycle, the re-use of the same instruments provides a measure of how much change has been achieved, of how much the gap between what is and what should be has been reduced.

Accessing the emotional literacy curriculum

The skills of emotional literacy can be learnt and the dimensions of emotional literacy that have been outlined in Chapter 2 provide the 'content' of the curriculum to be learned. This curriculum then needs to be made accessible to students. There are three layers in this process, all of which are necessary to achieve students' access to the emotional literacy curriculum. The first level is the whole school and it provides an ethos or context for the second and third levels, which are those of classrooms and working with individual students.

> It is meaningful to think of organisations, including whole schools, in terms of how emotionally literate they are (Sharp, 2001) – that is, the extent to which the emotional or affective sides of life and work are being acknowledged and how members of the organisation listen to each other and are listened to. Schools, like the individuals within them, vary in their levels of emotional literacy.

> However, since students spend the majority of their time in classrooms, the classroom is the more immediate context in which emotional literacy is fostered. The degree of emotional literacy in a classroom is profoundly influenced by the emotional literacy of the teacher as well as the curriculum being offered. It is also affected by the emotional tone of the classroom which is reflected in issues like co-operation rather than competition, the cohesiveness of the group, and the way in which conflicts are addressed.

> Finally, a classroom is made up of individual students, each with their unique genetic, family and personal experiences resulting in a group of people who exhibit the whole gamut of emotional literacy competences. An inclusive classroom is one that recognises and values these differences and attempts to provide a curriculum (social and emotional as well as academic) which is accessible to all and meets the needs of all.

Whole-school level

In attempting to raise emotional literacy levels, a school's first task is to carry out an audit or baseline of the current situation. This requires the collection of data. The standardised checklists provided here enable schools to evaluate present levels of emotional literacy using the Teacher Checklist. For this purpose, schools may well wish to track the progress of the school as a whole or of particular years or class groups. It could also be used as a measure of comparison between similar schools. Clearly the practicality of such an audit in terms of teacher or adult time is an important consideration, and this is likely to be achieved by sampling the school population.

Our experience in the trialling of these materials is that it is practical for teachers to complete the Teacher Checklist for all their students. As a general principle, the more students for whom checklists are completed and the more teachers who complete them, the more reliable the measure of the school's emotional literacy is likely to be.

Classroom level

At the classroom level, individual teachers may wish to use the checklists, particularly the Teacher Checklist, as a measure of how they have influenced levels of their class's emotional literacy over time. This may be after new arrangements have been introduced or after a curriculum-based intervention. This would be particularly useful if the Teacher Checklist were used in conjunction with another tool such as the *Individualised Classroom Environment Questionnaire* (Fraser, 1990) which measures how students perceive their classrooms.

Individual level

Research has shown that teachers are usually very skilled at reliably rank-ordering students on a variety of dimensions. However, it has also been shown that, in the emotional and behavioural dimension, there is a tendency to overlook shy and withdrawn students (that is, those who internalise problems) in comparison with aggressive students (that is, those who externalise problems). This is readily understandable since externalising behaviour problems are more disruptive and more directly challenge the self-image of the teacher.

It is for these reasons that the checklists, particularly the Teacher Checklist and possibly also the Parent Checklist, are especially useful as screening instruments to identify those students at risk, especially those who may otherwise be overlooked. They provide a more detailed source of data that sometimes complements and even 'surprises' more global impressions. For students already identified as being at risk, the Teacher and Parent Checklists provide a structured and focused reflection of not only how serious problems are (with reference to the cut-offs provided), but where precisely the problems may lie. Classroom curricular interventions, class topics for circle time and so on can be guided by this information.

Increasingly schools have become more inclusive and attempt to meet not only the academic needs of students but their social and emotional ones too. Often this involves small group work, and the Teacher Checklist is invaluable in helping teachers to achieve a balance of students making up the group and giving information to help focus the work of the group itself, for example on anger or anxiety management, social skills and empathy. In these small groups, or in individual situations, the Student Checklist is particularly valuable.

It should be noted that all self-administered questionnaires about oneself are subject to biases. When questionnaires are being completed for others to see, we tend, even as adults, to present ourselves in a favourable light. This is particularly true when the person for whom the checklist is being completed has a managerial or selection role, and is especially true of children and young people in relation to their teachers and parents. We tend to answer questions in ways that reflect ourselves not so much as we really believe ourselves to be but rather as we would like others to think of us. People often either inflate or downplay their qualities. We sometimes complete self-assessments in accordance with our ideal self rather than our real self-image. Self-ratings are difficult to interpret, especially in children and young people, so it is valuable to have ratings from teachers and parents with which to compare the self-ratings.

The foundation for emotional literacy depends upon the dimension we have labelled as 'self-awareness'. This is to do with recognising our own emotions, strengths and weaknesses, reactions to commonly occurring situations, etc. It is possible that a person with little self-awareness may give exactly the same answers on a self-rating instrument as a person who is very emotionally literate, simply because he or she is not self-aware. It is also possible that effective interventions could lead to a situation where scores after the intervention are actually worse than before the intervention if the effectiveness of that intervention has raised levels of self-awareness so that students now no longer rate themselves in either inflated or downgraded ways.

The Student Checklist is best used in very supportive environments that are non-judgemental, emotionally warm, and where the student feels valued and listened to. Since the views of significant other people are a very important part of the process of becoming more self-aware, it is extremely useful to help young people see how teachers and parents and possibly their peers see them. The use of the Student Checklist can be compared by the student with versions completed by teachers and parents, and this process may enable the identification of priority areas to address for targeting change. Students can thus be supported in raising their achievements in the area of emotional literacy and, consequently, in other areas of school and home life also.

As secondary school students experience a variety of teachers and subjects, it is important to look at the way students think, feel and behave in different contexts. In attempting to analyse patterns of intensity and frequency of behaviour, it is essential that independent views of the student should be sought from all the teachers involved. The *Behaviour Survey Checklist* (Jolly & McNamara, undated) and a computerised adaptation of this (*Pupil Behaviour Assessment System*; PBAS) are particularly useful instruments in seeing how students' attitudes and behaviour are influenced by context and also for identifying particular skills and competences that may be presenting difficulties across a range of different settings.

Chapter 4: Developing emotional and social competences

An intervention is likely to be more or less successful to the extent that it embraces all three levels outlined on pages 15 to 17 – whole school, classroom and individual student. Individuals' behaviour is, for practical purposes, a function of the interaction between what they bring to the situation and their current context. Lewin (1966) summarised this interactional nature of human behaviour in the equation: $B=f(PE)$, that is, behaviour (B) is a function (f) of the interaction of person (P) and the environment (E).

Generally speaking, this Guide does not address whole-school issues in depth, but there are clear links with a number of current initiatives that do address whole-school issues. Among these are the 'Healthy Schools' initiative (DfES, 1998), PSHE policies and curriculum, citizenship (QCA, 2002) and behaviour and assessment policies (Education Act, 1997). Similarly, other instruments are available that address emotional literacy aspects of the classroom, including those published instruments which measure the emotional literacy of adults and which are appropriate for teachers and other adults in the classroom and those which measure classroom environments such as the *Individualised Classroom Environment Questionnaire* (Fraser, 1990).

The purpose of individual student assessment is to target areas of strength and weakness with a view to intervening in some way to help the individual acquire those skills and competences that will enable him or her to access the curriculum, to develop self-worth and to play a constructive part in the community, both now within school and in the future as an adult in society.

Interventions are designed to produce change in *behaviour*. To achieve behaviour change will usually involve changes in *thinking* and in *emotion*. As an individual's behaviour is almost always the result of interactions between what the individual brings to the situation (their genetic make-up, history, personality, current skills and competences) and the nature of the context or environment, it is clear that interventions are unlikely to be successful unless they combine changes in the environment as well as changes within the individual student.

The interventions outlined in this Guide are underpinned by two important frameworks.

Framework 1: Three-stage interventions

The first framework is a modification of the traditional ABC framework derived from an analysis of B (Behaviour) in terms of A (Antecedents: those aspects of the environment that can be manipulated) and C (Consequences). Any successful intervention will involve the following three stages.

1. Environmental changes

The environment needs to be changed so that problematic behaviour is less likely and pro-social, co-operative behaviour is more likely. The environment or context can include:

- the physical environment of the classroom;
- the way the classroom is organised;
- the nature of the curriculum so that it becomes more relevant and meaningful to the student and one which is matched to the current skill levels of that student;
- the personal and professional characteristics of the teacher;
- the teacher's skills in classroom management and organisation.

The skill of the teacher is extremely important from the point of view of emotional literacy and has a vital role to play in enhancing the students' self-esteem, self-worth and sense of value. The litmus test of the whole-school ethos, of the climate of individual classrooms and of the skills and competences of the teacher is how all of these contribute to enhancing and maintaining the individual student's self-worth.

It has been seen earlier in the Guide that, in the field of emotional literacy, most bad behaviour is viewed as emotional in origin and that most inappropriate social behaviour is an attempt to preserve a sense of self-worth. We become emotional because we perceive what is happening to us as de-valuing us so that we no longer belong.

A common dimension to the interventions described in this Guide is a focus on how whole-school, classroom and teacher variables can better foster the self-worth of students. These variables are all grouped under the generic title of 'environmental changes' in the interventions section on page 45. (They are also known as the 'antecedents of behaviour'.)

2. Consequences

There is a fairly universally recognised law in psychology that our behaviour is influenced by its consequences. This law of reinforcement suggests that the probability of behaviour increases if it is rewarded, and conversely that it is lessened if the behaviour is punished. For a variety of mainly ethical reasons, rewarding appropriate behaviour is believed to be more effective than punishing inappropriate behaviour. It is particularly important for teachers and parents to notice appropriate behaviours and to acknowledge and reward them. Punishment simply represses poor behaviour, whereas rewards reinforce positive and appropriate behaviour so that these behaviours can replace inappropriate ones. For this to be successful, the teacher needs to have a sufficiently concrete vision of what behaviours are desired. For example, punishing Darren for squabbling and fighting with Agung does not teach him what we really want to see, namely to see him working co-operatively with Agung. However, rewarding him when he does work co-operatively makes such behaviour more likely. This highlights the importance of rewarding approximations and examples of more appropriate behaviour when they occur and trying to ignore, if possible, episodes of inappropriate behaviour.

In all the interventions included in the interventions section on page 45, there is a dimension labelled 'consequences'.

3. Teaching personal competences and skills

However, by focusing solely on the *antecedents* (through environmental manipulation) and the *consequences*, a fundamental aspect of behaviour change is still being ignored – namely, the direct teaching of the skills and competences needed to carry out more appropriate behaviours. In other areas of school learning, we do not just focus on the antecedents and consequences, but we start with a clear idea of *what* we are trying to teach, we devise *methods* to do this and give students plenty of *practice with feedback* to guide their performance. When it comes to emotional and social behaviour, however, we tend to leap into consequences. Many school behaviour policies are often no more than lists of good and bad consequences for good and bad behaviour. Just as in other areas of the curriculum, before we think of rewards and punishments, we should be asking these questions first:

- Does the student actually know what he or she is supposed to do?
- Does the student know what the rules of the game are?

Even when we have ensured that this is the case, simply knowing *what* to do is never sufficient to learn a new skill: we have to be shown *how* to do it by a more experienced and competent person. We then we have to *practise and receive feedback* to develop the skill until it becomes an automatic part of our repertoire.

So, in the area of behaviour and poor interpersonal skills, it is really only *after* we are sure that the student knows *what* to do, has been clearly shown *how* to do it, and has had sufficient *practice* at doing it, that we may need then to ensure that the student considers it worthwhile to use the new skill. 'Can't do it' may be replaced by 'won't do it' at this point and it is here that the motivational aspect of behaviour change becomes important, namely rewards and punishments ('sticks and carrots').

Framework 2: Teaching alternative strategies

It is teaching, rather than rewards and punishments, which is at the heart of a school's learning policies for literacy, numeracy, science and all the other subjects, and it should also be at the heart of emotional literacy interventions. However, it is much more difficult to establish what skills and competences the student needs to acquire in emotional literacy compared with the more traditional and academic areas of the school curriculum. The second of our frameworks is designed to help answer this question of what the student needs to be taught.

It starts by considering the question: 'Why do we do what we do?'. A variety of meanings can be attributed to the question 'Why?'. It can refer primarily to the *past* in the sense of what causes us to behave in the way we do. This could be due to our genetic make-up, our early childhood experiences, the modelling and ways of thinking and behaviour we have internalised from our parents, and the rewards and punishments we have received. In a sense we can do very little about the past – we cannot change it, we can only learn from it. In terms of generating change in emotions or behaviour, the past is not a particularly fruitful line of inquiry.

The 'Why?' can also refer to the *present*, particularly the current pressures on us from family, the nature of the school we attend with its expectations and demands, the norms and standards purveyed by the media and particularly pressure from peers. The present is rather more amenable to change than the past, and that is why we focus on environmental change and consequences in the interventions suggested on page 45.

It is the *future* that is most open to change. There is a sense of 'Why?' that is primarily future-oriented, understood in the sense of function, purpose or motive. 'Why, for what purpose, did you …?' is the most relevant question we can ask in educating for emotional literacy. Motive and emotion are clearly linked together. When we are in any social situation, our behaviour can be considered as a task or problem to be solved. It is the focus on what the person is trying to achieve, where they are trying to get to by doing what they do, that is the most significant aspect of our approach to emotional literacy. This approach considers what is the meaning or purpose of the behaviour. We have seen that the hallmark of emotional literacy is that it considers emotions/feelings to be central to understanding what we do and why we do it. Our motives are fundamentally emotional.

Understanding the purpose of behaviour

The fundamental need to 'belong' is central to our being human. Of course, we share basic physiological needs with the rest of the animal kingdom. We will, like them, react with the biological mechanisms of fight, flight and playing dead in our evolutionary drive for survival. But, for human beings, survival is not just about food, warmth and shelter. It is about belonging – so we react with those same evolutionary mechanisms for survival when our built-in scanning mechanism picks up threats to our sense of belonging, threats to our emotional survival. As self-reflecting conscious beings, our physiological responses are accompanied by the feelings or emotions of anger (fight), anxiety (flight) or depression (playing dead). The protection of our sense of 'belonging' is the major motive of our existence and often the explanation for our behaviour.

What does belonging mean in practice? It means we perceive that we play a significant part in the human community as experienced in our immediate family, school and workplace. To play a significant part in a community means to feel that we are of value and have self-worth – at its basic level, that we are both loved and lovable. The task for every human being is to enhance and maintain his or her own sense of worth and lovableness and, at the same time, maintain the worth of other people. Our own and other people's sense of worth are intimately and inseparably bound together.

So what then is the explanation of 'bad' behaviour or, in other words, behaviour that destroys human community and interpersonal relationships? Emotional literacy focuses on *emotional* reasons.

When our basic human survival is threatened, we sense a threat to our belonging, to our self-worth, self-confidence, value or lovableness. We respond with a biologically built-in response. Which of the three biological strategies to survive is used will depend on a number of factors, but one will be used and so the person will experience anger, anxiety or depression. Since we do not like these emotions, we will do almost anything to get rid of them. In fact, they are precisely there to force us to act in order to survive. They impel us to get rid of feelings of anger by attacking, physically or verbally; to get rid of anxiety by running away or withdrawing; to get rid of depression by shutting down all emotions and playing dead emotionally. However, we can also get rid of these feelings, not by only doing what biologically we are being driven to do, but by simply 'suppressing' the aversive feelings so that we stop feeling them. Things like alcohol, nicotine, drugs, sex, shopping and exercise can become addictive ways of reducing feelings of anger, anxiety and depression. While they can be effective in the short term, in the longer term they can be disastrous emotionally, socially and sometimes physically as well.

But we are not just emotional, we are rational creatures as well. Reason is about long-term problem-solving, assessing the pros and cons of our actions and the long-term effects on our belonging and self-worth. There is therefore a tension between the short-term pull of emotions and weighing up the long-term effects of our actions by rational thinking. Emotional literacy is about how we resolve that tension.

Poor behaviours are short-term solutions which do not ultimately increase or maintain our sense of worth or belonging, but reduce them. They destroy community by denying other people's sense of value and dignity. Judgemental attitudes that question our personal worth (for instance, 'You are bad, naughty, lazy, stupid, incapable, unmotivated, selfish, etc.') emerge as a fundamental threat to self-worth and are extremely effective at provoking a perception of being seriously threatened and attacked.

The communicative function of behaviour

One way teachers can non-judgementally view emotionally illiterate, anti-social behaviour is to adopt a position that views the majority of behaviour, if not all behaviour, as fundamentally good in *intention*. The real purpose of all our behaviour is our physical and, more importantly, our emotional survival. In other words what we are trying to do, even in our bad behaviour, is to protect our legitimate needs but the means, the strategies, are sometimes harmful to other people and to ourselves. (Morality tends not to be about ends, but about means.)

So, faced with poor behaviour, we need to adopt a detective-style approach – to be curious about what might be the real motive for the behaviour. Rather than using the judgemental question 'Why *did* you do that?', we can quizzically ask, in a non-judgemental manner, 'Why, *for what purpose*?'.

● **EXAMPLE**

When John hits George in the corridor, we need to ask, 'Why, for what purpose?'. What was he really trying to achieve with that behaviour? Our first answer is that he was trying to hurt George, which indeed he did. But hurting others is not a legitimate need, so we have to ask again, 'Why, *for what purpose*, did he want to hurt him?'. We then discover that George called John's mother an unpleasant name, and now we have a legitimate need for John, which is to protect his mother's good name and convey that he really does not find her being called a derogatory name acceptable behaviour. Those are his rights and his needs and it is legitimate that John should convey them to George. However, the way John chose to convey them was anti-social and destructive and the effects of such behaviour frequently rebound upon himself.

So the task of the teachers and the school is to try to work out what legitimate need a bad behaviour is trying to achieve. This is sometimes called the 'communicative function of behaviour', which is another way of saying 'What does the behaviour really mean, what is the need that is being protected?'. Experience tells us that there are a number of legitimate needs that reflect or express our need to belong. For example, the need to belong, to think oneself to be lovable and to have self-worth are experienced in school situations as the need for:

- attention
- justice/reparation
- power and control (issues of choice/task avoidance)
- acceptance and affiliation (friendships and companions)
- access to tangible resources (for example, classroom equipment)
- stimulation (avoidance of boredom)
- expression of self.

Teaching alternative strategies

Having established why the student behaved in a certain way, the next task is to teach alternative strategies that achieve the same end. In John's case, in the example above, this would be a replacement behaviour that serves the same function but involves the use of assertiveness skills rather than aggression. Such skills are often language-based skills. Emotionally illiterate people frequently have very poor pragmatic language skills. Hence the emotional literacy curriculum begins with labelling and discriminating between emotions. So, to get John to the point where he can use functionally equivalent alternative strategies, we may first need to teach him pre-skills that are necessary for him to carry out the more complex task. As in every other area of the curriculum, in the emotional literacy curriculum it is essential to:

- know where we want the learner to get to;
- find out their current level of the target skill;
- ascertain the sequence of sub-skills required;
- decide what is the next step to be taught.

The difficulty is that, because these are emotional issues, the tension between the demands of the here and now and the longer-term view of defending our sense of belonging in pro-social ways can be very strong. When we are physiologically aroused, our emotions can 'hijack' us and take over. So, as well as the replacement behaviours, we may have to teach 'coping skills' which involves teaching tactics and strategies to control escalating levels of emotional arousal. All children and young people need to learn how to control their own physiology. Examples of such strategies include self-talk, distraction, breathing exercises, relaxation, visualisation and meditation. Bad behaviour is viewed in all these strategies as a response to stress, where stress is defined as those situations where our ability and competences to meet the need to belong are being fundamentally questioned.

The process of teaching emotional literacy

All the interventions in this Guide are offered as suggestions to enable teachers and other adults to support the student. Teachers may find it helpful to follow the steps below.

Step 1 is to identify what skills and competences the student already possesses.

Step 2 requires the identification of areas of weakness and prioritisation of these so that the focus is on workable interventions and achievable goals.

Step 3 is to explore whether there are some exceptions to the rule, that is some situations where the poor behaviour does not occur or occurs with much less intensity or frequency. This is a very important part of the assessment process since the absence of poor behaviour (or less intense behaviour) in these situations indicates that in that context or environment legitimate needs are not perceived to be under such attack. Examining what is different in the exceptional environment often provides clues as to how other environments, where the behaviour is problematic, can be modified to make that behaviour less likely.

Step 4 is to establish the function of the behaviour by asking what legitimate need the student's behaviour is trying to solve.

Step 5 is to generate alternative ways of achieving the same end and to make sure that the student has the necessary skills to do so.

Step 6 is to explain, model and demonstrate new behaviours and to explain why and how the new behaviours will better meet the student's needs.

Step 7 is to work on the skills and competences together.

Step 8 is to set up safe situations, in simulation or role-play, for the student to practise the new skills and for the teacher to provide feedback.

Step 9 is to get the student to practise in the real world, in real life. Once within the student's repertoire, its very effectiveness should mean that the skill is self-maintaining, but there may be a need for incentives and rewards for the student to continue to view the use of these skills as worthwhile.

Chapter 5: Administering and scoring the checklists

The three standardised checklists included in this Guide help to determine how best to support students and are designed to foster inclusion. The checklists can be used for a variety of purposes, such as:

- identification and screening of individual students;
- evaluation of general or specific interventions;
- curriculum planning.

Each checklist should take no more than 10 minutes to complete. It is advisable to complete the checklists after the first term when the teacher has become more familiar with each student.

Student Checklist

The Student Checklist has 25 items and assesses the emotional literacy of students based on the views of individuals themselves.

This version is most appropriate for use in small groups or individual counselling environments after trust has been established. It is less appropriate at whole-school or classroom levels (see page 17 for more about this version of the checklist).

Teacher Checklist

The Teacher Checklist has 20 items and assesses the emotional literacy of students based on the views of their teachers, or other adults in the school.

This version is most useful at whole-school or classroom levels to act as:

- an audit;
- a baseline and post-intervention measure;
- a screening device to identify students at risk.

The Teacher Checklist is also important as a baseline and post-intervention measure in small group and individual situations and as a way of facilitating student self-awareness.

Parent Checklist

The Parent Checklist has 25 items and assesses the emotional literacy of students based on the views of parents or primary carers at home.

This version can be used as part of an audit or screening procedure but, for practical reasons, its most likely use will be for students attending social skills or anger/anxiety management groups or individual counselling situations. In counselling sessions, the use of the Parent Checklist would complement the views of the Teacher Checklist to help an individual student understand how significant people see him or her and thus to establish some priority targets for intervention. Careful preparation and negotiation with parents is necessary to ensure that the purpose of collecting the information is clearly explained and that it is understood that it will be only used to support their child in becoming more emotionally literate.

Administering the checklists

Before the forms are completed it is important that respondents (whether they are teachers, parents or students) understand the nature of the checklist they are about to complete, and why they are being asked to complete it.

They should be assured that the answers they give will be treated in strictest confidence and that named responses will not be shared with any classmates or members of school staff other than those directly involved with analysing or acting on results.

As with any checklists of this nature they should be completed in a quiet setting, where the respondent can work free from interruption and without being overlooked.

Student Checklist

1. Ensure that students complete the section at the top of the form which asks for name, date, class details and sex.

2. Ensure that the students understand how to complete the checklist, by talking through the example on the form before they start.

3. Once they have filled in the personal details and indicated that they understand how to fill in the checklist, the students should then complete the checklists independently.

Teacher Checklist

1. Ensure that the personal details including the student's name, date, year group and sex are completed on each form.

2. The checklist comprises a series of statements. In order to assess the emotional literacy of the student, simply tick one of four boxes to indicate how well each statement describes how the student generally is – the respondent indicates if the statement is 'very true', 'somewhat true', 'not really true' or 'not at all true' of the student being rated.

Parent Checklist

The Parent Checklist is completed in the same way as the Teacher Checklist. Instructions are found at the back of this Guide and should be photocopied and sent to the student's home together with the checklist. Alternatively, you may prefer to use your own wording in a covering letter and send this with the checklist.

Scoring the checklists

To obtain an emotional literacy rating for the student:

1. Each item in the checklist is rated from 1 to 4. Use the appropriate scoring key provided in the back of this Guide to score each item. Follow the instructions on the key. Scores can be transferred to the optional Student Score Sheet, if desired.

2. Overall (total) emotional literacy scores are obtained for all the checklists by simply summing the scores for each item. A higher score indicates better emotional literacy.

3. For the Teacher and Parent Checklists, additional subscale scores can be obtained using the scoring keys in the back of this Guide. Thus the following scores can be obtained:

Score Checklist	Overall emotional literacy score	Self-awareness subscale score	Self-regulation subscale score	Motivation subscale score	Empathy subscale score	Social skills subscale score
Student	✔					
Teacher	✔	✔	✔	✔	✔	✔
Parent	✔	✔	✔	✔	✔	✔

Interpreting the checklists

There are a number of important things to bear in mind when interpreting the results.

These checklists do not objectively measure behaviour, competences or skills – they measure perceptions. It should also be noted that all self-administered questionnaires about oneself are subject to biases. When questionnaires are being completed for other people to look at, we tend, even as adults, to present ourselves in a very favourable light. People also often either inflate or downplay their qualities. We sometimes complete self-assessments not in accordance with our real self-image but in accordance with our ideal self. Self-ratings of oneself are difficult to interpret, especially in children and young people. It is therefore valuable to have ratings from teachers and parents with which to compare the self-assessments. See pages 16, 17 and 25 for further information about the use of the checklists.

When people complete questionnaires or checklists about other people, there is a tendency to succumb to what is known as the 'halo effect'. This means that, once someone holds a particular view, there is a tendency to carry on thinking in that way. For example, in an otherwise emotionally literate student, because we see that student as generally having good emotional literacy, we may not notice particular weaknesses. Alternatively, and possibly more significantly, we may not notice any strengths in a student who is causing major concerns. It is partly for this reason that some items in the checklists are worded positively and some negatively. This also helps to reduce the tendency for a 'response bias', when we simply get into the habit of putting ticks in the same column. Having positive and negative items all mixed up helps to make us consider each item on its merits.

It is not the purpose of these checklists to label students. Since labelling can act against inclusion, it can only be justified when it leads to positive and empowering action. Generally, when used for screening, baselining or evaluating, these checklists are not concerned with individual students as such but more with classroom and school averages or distributions. When we are interested in individual students, the purpose of administering these instruments is to help us act and to foster inclusion, not to label.

Comparing scores with a nationally representative sample

Chapter 6 provides more detailed information about the national sample, the reliability and validity of the scales, and the differences in scores by year group and gender.

You can compare your students' scores with those of a nationally representative sample by using the cut-offs presented in Tables 1 to 3. The cut-offs have been derived from the norms of the standardisation sample. The tables divide the scores into bands as follows and these can be used both for the overall emotional literacy scores and for subscale scores where they are available:

Score band	Percentage of students falling within a band	Description	In need of intervention?
1	10	Well below average	Yes
2	15	Below average	
3	50	Average	No
4	15	Above average	
5	10	Well above average	

Students in score band 1 have scores in the bottom 10 per cent of students in the national sample, while those in score band 5 have scores in the top 10 per cent of students in the national sample. Students in score band 3 have scores in the middle 50 per cent of students in the national sample.

- Therefore, those students with scores falling in score band 1 have scores well below the national average and should be flagged up as having potential problems with emotional literacy: they may be in particular need of some form of further intervention, such as those suggested in this Guide.
- Students scoring in bands 2 to 4 are scoring around the average compared to students in the national sample, whereas scores within score band 5 are well above average. Students in score bands 2 to 5 are not in particular need of further intervention but might, nevertheless, benefit from being involved in such activities.

It should be noted that these checklists are intended for screening students with particular problems in emotional literacy, rather than identifying those with particularly strong emotional literacy skills. The checklists are sensitive to differences between low scorers and others, but are less sensitive to differences amongst high scorers.

Table 1: Student Checklist – cut-offs for score bands for the overall emotional literacy score

Score band	Description	Score range
1	Well below average	61 or below
2	Below average	62–66
3	Average	67–78
4	Above average	79–83
5	Well above average	84 or above

Table 2: Teacher Checklist – cut-offs for score bands for the overall emotional literacy score and subscale scores

Score band	Description	Score ranges for overall emotional literacy and subscale scores					
		Overall	*Self-awareness*	*Self-regulation*	*Motivation*	*Empathy*	*Social skills*
1	Well below average	42 or below	8 or below	6 or below	6 or below	8 or below	9 or below
2	Below average	43–50	9–10	7–8	7–8	9–10	10–11
3	Average	51–69	11–13	9–14	9–13	11–14	12–14
4	Above average	70–75	14	15	14–15	15	15
5	Well above average	76 or above	15–16	16	16	16	16

Table 3: Parent Checklist – cut-offs for score bands for the overall emotional literacy score and subscale scores

Score band	Description	Score ranges for overall emotional literacy and subscale scores					
		Overall	*Self-awareness*	*Self-regulation*	*Motivation*	*Empathy*	*Social skills*
1	Well below average	60 or below	10 or below	8 or below	9 or below	11 or below	14 or below
2	Below average	61–67	11–12	9–11	10–11	12–13	15–16
3	Average	68–80	13–14	12–15	12–16	14–17	17–19
4	Above average	81–86	15	16–17	17	18	20
5	Well above average	87 or above	16–20	18–20	18–20	19–20	

Use of the scores in schools

The five dimensions used in these materials are subsets of the more global concept of emotional literacy. They are not completely independent of each other and there is considerable overlap between them. However, evidence from the standardisation (see page 39) demonstrates that the Teacher and Parent Checklists do discriminate between the subscales adequately and it is therefore likely that students will show some variation between the subscales.

Generally speaking, it will be the overall emotional literacy score that will contribute to the judgement that a student requires support to become more emotionally literate. Teacher observations of the student and of peer reactions to the student will be part of that judgement and decisions about the need to intervene should not be made on the basis of the results of the checklists alone.

However, having established the need for some intervention, the profile of subscales can help the teacher to decide what competences and skills might be a priority area to work on, and may also help in the decisions about the composition of small groups of students for differentiated activities. Should a student score significantly less on one dimension compared with all the other subscales, this might suggest interventions for those items within that dimension as a priority.

Although the dimensions are not ordered hierarchically, it would appear that the ability to know and label one's own emotions is a crucial foundation for the rest of emotional literacy. So, if a student scores low on that dimension (self-awareness), it is strongly recommended that work should first be carried out in that area. An example profile is shown below.

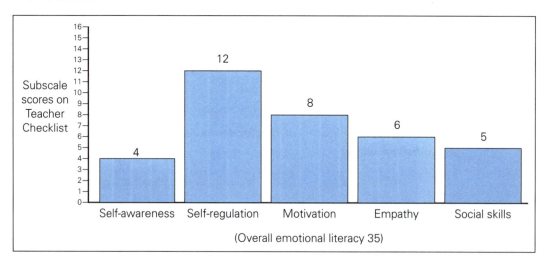

(Overall emotional literacy 35)

Alternatively, the problem behaviour (related perhaps to self-regulation) may itself indicate a priority area. For example, a student may be placing him or herself at considerable risk of exclusion owing to aggressive behaviour that derives from an inability to manage angry feelings. An example profile is shown below.

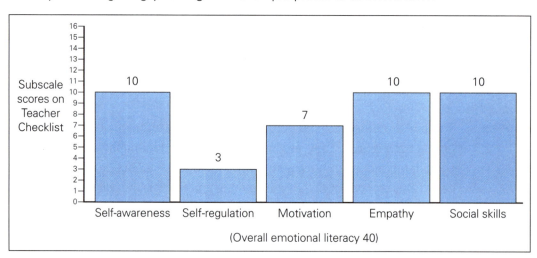

(Overall emotional literacy 40)

Chapter 6: Technical information

Development of the emotional literacy checklists

The items in the checklists were generated by multidisciplinary teams working on the emotional literacy initiatives in schools in Southampton. Early editions of the checklists were trialled in a sample of schools around Southampton in December 2002. The analysis of these early editions informed the development of versions used with the standardisation sample.

Items in the final versions of the checklists were initially developed and selected primarily because they were seen to be appropriate and adequate measures of each of the five proposed underlying dimensions of emotional literacy, as defined by Goleman (1996). However, there was also a recognition of the practical need to keep scales short, while also ensuring that there were sufficient numbers of items to be reliable and to discriminate sufficiently between students, particularly those scoring towards the lower end of the range of possible scores. Time taken to complete the checklists was recognised as being of particular importance for teachers.

The standardisation sample

Please note that figures for both the Student Checklist (ages 11 to 16) and the Pupil Checklist (ages 7 to 11) are presented here since the analysis was conducted on the whole data set. The Pupil Checklist is presented in a sister publication, *Emotional Literacy: Assessment and Intervention – Ages 7 to 11*.

Standardisation of the emotional literacy checklists took place in a randomly selected nationally representative sample of primary and secondary schools in England in March 2003 and was carried out by the National Foundation for Educational Research. Schools were asked to provide completed checklists for students aged from 7 to 16. In recognition of the workload implications for teachers who were involved in national tests, in Years 6, 9 and 11 (England), only Pupil/Student Checklists were completed, whereas for the other year groups Teacher and Parent Checklists were also completed. (Age bands in the tables overlap as they are based on year groups.)

Pupil Checklist (ages 7 to 11)

The sample that completed the Pupil Checklist comprised 732 pupils from 28 schools, of whom 54 per cent were male. Table 4 shows the numbers of pupils (and percentages of the sample) from each age group sampled.

Table 4: Total numbers of pupils at each age who completed the Pupil Checklist

Age	Frequency	Percentage
7–8	195	27
8–9	177	24
9–10	191	26
10–11	169	23
Total	732	100

Student Checklist (ages 11 to 16)

The sample that completed the Student Checklist comprised 967 students from 26 schools, of whom 49 per cent were male. Table 5 shows the numbers and percentages of students from each age group sampled.

Table 5: Total numbers of students at each age who completed the Student Checklist

Age	Frequency	Percentage
11–12	205	21
12–13	209	22
13–14	194	20
14–15	174	18
15–16	183	19
Total	965	100

Note: Two cases had no year groups assigned.

Teacher Checklist

The Teacher Checklist was completed for 449 pupils and students in total, from 34 schools, of whom 51 per cent were male. Table 6 shows the numbers of pupils and students (and percentages of the sample) for whom the teachers completed checklists.

Table 6: Total numbers of students for whom the Teacher Checklist was completed

Age of pupils/students	Frequency	Percentage
7–8	70	16
8–9	69	15
9–10	80	18
11–12	90	20
12–13	80	18
14–15	60	13
Total	449	100

Parent Checklist

The Parent Checklist was completed for 569 pupils and students in total, from 35 schools, of whom 47 per cent were male. Table 7 shows the numbers of pupils and students (and percentages of the sample) for whom parents completed checklists.

Table 7: Total numbers of students for whom the Parent Checklist was completed

Age of pupils/students	Frequency	Percentage
7–8	111	20
8–9	99	17
9–10	101	18
11–12	89	16
12–13	95	17
14–15	73	13
Total	568	100

Note: One case had no year group assigned.

Reliability

The reliability analysis of the standardisation data addressed the extent to which items in the emotional literacy checklists were measuring the same underlying concept. The reliability of overall emotional literacy and subscale scores was assessed for Student, Teacher and Parent Checklists.

Reliability was assessed using Cronbach's Alpha. The range of values for this statistic is from 0 to 1, with a higher score indicating a reliable scale. Scores of around 0.70, for the majority of scales within each checklist, were assumed to be indicative of adequate reliability in this analysis.

Tables 8 to 10 show Cronbach's Alpha for each of the checklists. The results show that, while the majority of subscales in the Teacher and Parent Checklists were reliable, the subscales (such as self-awareness) in the Student Checklist were not. (See page 17 for more information about the use of self-rating scales and their reliability.) However, the reliabilities for the overall emotional literacy scales were sufficiently reliable for Student, Teacher and Parent Checklists. The decision to provide subscale scores and cut-offs for the Teacher and Parent Checklists but not for the Student Checklists was based on these findings.

Table 8: Student Checklist – reliability

Scales	Number of items	Cronbach's Alpha
Self-awareness	5	0.47
Self-regulation	5	0.58
Motivation	5	0.68
Empathy	5	0.56
Social skills	5	0.58
Overall emotional literacy	25	0.75

Table 9: Teacher Checklist – reliability

Scales	Number of items	Cronbach's Alpha
Self-awareness	4	0.70
Self-regulation	4	0.88
Motivation	4	0.87
Empathy	4	0.82
Social skills	4	0.82
Overall emotional literacy	20	0.94

Table 10: Parent Checklist – reliability

Scales	Number of items	Cronbach's Alpha
Self-awareness	5	0.58
Self-regulation	5	0.74
Motivation	5	0.74
Empathy	5	0.58
Social skills	5	0.75
Overall emotional literacy	25	0.87

Validity

The analysis of the standardisation data concerned with the validity of the checklists focused on exploring the extent to which the five dimensions of emotional literacy proposed by Goleman (1996) were evident in the data. As the subscales for students were found to be unreliable, this analysis was restricted to the Teacher and Parent Checklists only.

Validity was assessed in two ways:

- by examining the patterns of correlations between each item in the checklist with the subscale and overall emotional literacy scores;
- by revealing the underlying dimensions of the patterns of scores in the standardisation data using principal components factor analysis.

Correlations between items and total scale scores

Tables 11 and 12 present Pearson Product Moment Correlations between each item in each checklist and the subscale and overall emotional literacy scores. This statistic can range from 0, indicating no relationship, to 1 indicating a perfect relationship between two variables.

The tables show that the majority of items in the subscales were most highly correlated with other items in the same subscale. This pattern of results provides evidence that items in the subscales were measuring the same underlying concepts. The tables also show that items were highly correlated with the overall emotional literacy scores. These results indicate that each of the items within the subscales was also measuring some aspect of emotional literacy as one overall construct rather than just separate concepts of social skills or self-awareness.

Principal components factor analysis

Factor analysis is a collection of techniques which examine the correlations between a set of variables to identify those variables that are highly correlated. Groups of related variables or factors are thought to reflect underlying processes that have created the correlations between variables. Thus, factor analysis allows the factor structure of a set of variables to be uncovered. Principal components factor analysis was the technique used in this study as it is straightforward conceptually and mathematically and only rarely leads to drawing conclusions that are different from other types of factor analysis. An oblimin rotation was used to allow the factors to correlate, as significant correlations were found between the different subscales.

The results are presented in the form of factor loadings that measure the extent to which the variance in each item is explained by each factor. An important test of the analysis is interpretability: factor structure is most interpretable when certain conditions are met. These are when each variable loads strongly on one, and only one, factor and when most loadings are high and low.

Tables 13 and 14 on pages 37 and 38 present the results of the factor analyses of the Teacher and Parent Checklists. The results show that the data fit quite well with the five

Table 11: Teacher Checklist – correlations of items with scales

Scale	Checklist item	SA	SR	M	E	SS	Overall
Self-awareness (SA)	Finds it hard to accept constructive criticism and feedback.	0.67	0.69	0.47	0.54	0.46	0.68
	Can recognise the early signs of becoming angry.	0.76	0.47	0.47	0.43	0.44	0.60
	Can name or label his/her feelings.	0.74	0.29	0.45	0.37	0.44	0.54
	Is aware of his/her own strengths and qualities.	0.75	0.36	0.55	0.40	0.52	0.60
Self-regulation (SR)	Is liable to sulk if doesn't get his/her own way.	0.59	0.86	0.49	0.61	0.47	0.73
	Remains calm and composed when loses or 'fails' at something.	0.59	0.85	0.50	0.57	0.43	0.71
	Loses temper when loses at a game or in a competition.	0.46	0.87	0.49	0.62	0.39	0.69
	When things go wrong, immediately denies that it is his/her fault or blames others.	0.56	0.85	0.62	0.67	0.52	0.79
Motivation (M)	When starts a task or assignment, usually follows it through to completion.	0.59	0.48	0.88	0.53	0.55	0.73
	Gives up easily when faced with something difficult.	0.58	0.58	0.81	0.51	0.53	0.73
	Does things when they need to be done.	0.63	0.51	0.87	0.56	0.54	0.75
	Leaves things to the last minute.	0.48	0.50	0.83	0.50	0.46	0.68
Empathy (E)	Listens to other people's point of view in a discussion or argument.	0.64	0.66	0.64	0.78	0.60	0.80
	Is intolerant of people who are different from him/her.	0.37	0.41	0.39	0.75	0.26	0.53
	Is insensitive to the feelings of others.	0.52	0.63	0.55	0.88	0.50	0.74
	Is very critical of others' shortcomings.	0.49	0.63	0.44	0.82	0.42	0.67
Social skills (SS)	Laughs and smiles when it is appropriate to do so.	0.54	0.45	0.44	0.47	0.81	0.63
	Makes the right kind of eye contact when interacting with others.	0.62	0.45	0.56	0.46	0.83	0.69
	Has a sense of humour and fun that is used appropriately.	0.45	0.34	0.45	0.36	0.83	0.57
	Is disliked by many of his/her peers.	0.44	0.49	0.51	0.47	0.76	0.64

Table 12: Parent Checklist – correlations of items with scales

Scale	Checklist item	SA	SR	M	E	SS	Overall
Self-awareness (SA)	Is easily hurt by what others say about him/her.	0.56	0.25	0.16	0.17	0.21	0.35
	Can name or label his/her feelings.	0.62	0.25	0.27	0.22	0.33	0.44
	Is aware of his/her own strengths and weaknesses.	0.66	0.30	0.37	0.30	0.27	0.50
	Tends to have feelings of self-doubt/insecurity.	0.63	0.30	0.36	0.20	0.24	0.45
	Can recognise the early signs of becoming angry.	0.58	0.36	0.30	0.31	0.17	0.46
Self-regulation (SR)	Rushes into things without really thinking.	0.36	0.64	0.52	0.40	0.11	0.57
	Is quick tempered and aggressive.	0.37	0.72	0.41	0.47	0.29	0.63
	Is liable to sulk if doesn't get his/her own way.	0.27	0.70	0.32	0.34	0.19	0.53
	When things go wrong, immediately denies that it is his/her fault or blames others.	0.34	0.73	0.39	0.44	0.24	0.61
	Is a bad loser.	0.37	0.71	0.35	0.41	0.24	0.59
Motivation (M)	When starts a task, usually follows it through to completion.	0.30	0.27	0.73	0.27	0.18	0.49
	Gives up easily when things aren't perfect.	0.43	0.52	0.70	0.36	0.21	0.62
	Leaves things to the last minute.	0.24	0.45	0.69	0.26	0.13	0.53
	Keeps trying even when faced with something difficult.	0.35	0.33	0.70	0.26	0.26	0.54
	Seems able to shut out distractions when needs to focus.	0.37	0.35	0.70	0.29	0.20	0.54
Empathy (E)	Listens to other people's point of view in a discussion or argument.	0.44	0.51	0.48	0.59	0.23	0.61
	Is insensitive to the feelings of others.	0.21	0.29	0.22	0.66	0.16	0.41
	Is very critical of others' shortcomings.	0.20	0.36	0.22	0.65	0.25	0.45
	Is tolerant of people who are different from him/her.	0.09	0.18	0.12	0.54	0.16	0.30
	Gets annoyed when other people get things wrong.	0.24	0.45	0.26	0.62	0.19	0.47
Social skills (SS)	Mixes with other children.	0.32	0.18	0.12	0.28	0.70	0.42
	Can make friends again after a row.	0.25	0.19	0.18	0.18	0.60	0.36
	Spends too much time alone.	0.22	0.16	0.18	0.17	0.76	0.38
	Is liked by a lot of people.	0.35	0.28	0.30	0.28	0.68	0.51
	Finds it difficult to make new friends.	0.32	0.31	0.20	0.29	0.82	0.51

Table 13: Teacher Checklist – principal components factor analysis with oblimin rotation, pattern matrix

Scale	Checklist item	Factors				
		1	2	3	4	5
Self-awareness	Finds it hard to accept constructive criticism and feedback.		-0.72			
	Can recognise the early signs of becoming angry.				0.72	
	Can name or label his/her feelings.				0.74	
	Is aware of his/her own strengths and qualities.				0.58	
Self-regulation	Is liable to sulk if doesn't get his/her own way.		-0.81			
	Remains calm and composed when loses or 'fails' at something.		-0.80			
	Loses temper when loses at a game or in a competition.		-0.78			
	When things go wrong, immediately denies that it is his/her fault or blames others.		-0.57			
Motivation	When starts a task or assignment, usually follows it through to completion.	0.76				
	Gives up easily when faced with something difficult.	0.64				
	Does things when they need to be done.	0.70				
	Leaves things to the last minute.	0.84				
Empathy	Listens to other people's point of view in a discussion or argument.					
	Is intolerant of people who are different from him/her.					0.92
	Is insensitive to the feelings of others.					0.69
	Is very critical of others' shortcomings.					0.60
Social skills	Laughs and smiles when it is appropriate to do so.			0.78		
	Makes the right kind of eye contact when interacting with others.			0.65		
	Has a sense of humour and fun that is used appropriately.			0.91		
	Is disliked by many of his/her peers.			0.59		

Note: Loadings below 0.40 have not been printed. Extraction method = forced to extract 5 factors. Percentage of variance explained = 70.8%.

Table 14: Parent Checklist – principal components factor analysis with oblimin rotation, pattern matrix

Scale	Checklist item	Factors					
		1	2	3	4	5	6
Self-awareness	Is easily hurt by what others say about him/her.				-0.75		
	Can name or label his/her feelings.					-0.65	
	Is aware of his/her own strengths and weaknesses.					-0.56	
	Tends to have feelings of self-doubt/insecurity.				-0.72		
	Can recognise the early signs of becoming angry.					-0.56	
Self-regulation	Rushes into things without really thinking.	0.31		-0.40			
	Is quick tempered and aggressive.	0.55					
	Is liable to sulk if doesn't get his/her own way.	0.76					
	When things go wrong, immediately denies that it is his/her fault or blames others.	0.60					
	Is a bad loser.	0.72					
Motivation	When starts a task, usually follows it through to completion.			-0.83			
	Gives up easily when things aren't perfect.			-0.41			
	Leaves things to the last minute.			-0.59			
	Keeps trying even when faced with something difficult.			-0.68			
	Seems able to shut out distractions when needs to focus.			-0.69			
Empathy	Listens to other people's point of view in a discussion or argument.					-0.42	
	Is insensitive to the feelings of others.						0.75
	Is very critical of others' shortcomings.						0.48
	Is tolerant of people who are different from him/her.						0.62
	Gets annoyed when other people get things wrong.	0.58					
Social skills	Mixes with other children.		0.70				
	Can make friends again after a row.		0.57				
	Spends too much time alone.		0.76				
	Is liked by a lot of people.		0.62				
	Finds it difficult to make new friends.		0.78				

Note: Loadings below 0.40 have not been printed. Extraction method = Eigen values of 1 and over. Percentage of variance explained = 53.9%.

underlying dimensions proposed by Goleman (1996), particularly in the Teacher Checklist where just one item in the self-awareness subscale loads highly on a different factor from the other items in the scale. In addition just one item in the empathy subscale does not load above 0.40 on any factor. Although the factor structure fits less well for the Parent Checklist, most items load on the same factor as other items in the subscale. Self-awareness is again perhaps the most problematic subscale, with two items that appear to measure aspects of self-worth loading highly on a separate factor on which no other items load. Future research might use these results to investigate ways of developing some items in the existing scales to achieve a simpler factor structure.

The patterns of results found in the correlation tables and in the results of the factor analyses support the validity of Goleman's five-dimensional structure of emotional literacy (1996). This evidence provided the rationale for calculating subscale scores for the Teacher and Parent Checklists.

Differences in scores by year

The overall emotional literacy scores and subscale scores in different years were compared in the national sample. There was no statistically significant trend in scores by age for most of the scales. The mean overall emotional literacy score showed a small decrease between the ages of 11 and 15, but this difference was not sufficiently large in practical terms to warrant the provision of separate cut-offs for score bands by year.

Differences in scores by gender

Tables 15 to 17 compare results for males and females. On average teachers scored females higher than males. The overall teacher score was around 7 points higher for females than for males. The teacher ratings for the subscales were also higher for females and the differences were statistically significant. Parents also scored females higher than males and the differences were statistically significant for the overall score and for self-regulation, motivation and social skills. Girls' ratings on the Student Checklist were on average slightly higher than for boys, but this difference was small and not statistically significant.

Table 15: Student Checklist – sex differences

		Overall emotional literacy
Male	Mean	72.4
	SD*	9.0
Female	Mean	72.7
	SD	8.2
Total	Mean	72.6
	SD	8.6
Mean sex difference		0.3

*Standard deviation

Table 16: Teacher Checklist – sex differences

		Overall emotional literacy	Self-awareness	Self-regulation	Motivation	Empathy	Social skills
Male	Mean	55.5	11.1	10.4	10.2	11.5	12.5
	SD*	11.7	2.3	3.5	3.3	3.0	2.4
Female	Mean	62.8	12.0	11.9	12.3	12.9	13.5
	SD	11.3	2.2	3.1	3.0	2.6	2.4
Total	Mean	59.1	11.6	11.1	11.2	12.2	13.0
	SD	12.1	2.3	3.4	3.3	2.9	2.5
Mean sex difference**		**7.3**	**0.9**	**1.5**	**2.0**	**1.4**	**1.0**

*Standard deviation **Differences that are statistically significant are shown in bold*

Table 17: Parent Checklist – sex differences

		Overall emotional literacy	Self-awareness	Self-regulation	Motivation	Empathy	Social skills
Male	Mean	71.6	13.3	12.7	13.0	14.9	17.2
	SD*	10.4	2.6	3.2	3.2	2.6	2.5
Female	Mean	74.6	13.5	13.5	14.5	15.3	17.7
	SD	9.8	2.2	3.4	2.8	2.7	2.4
Total	Mean	73.2	13.4	13.1	13.8	15.2	17.5
	SD	10.2	2.4	3.3	3.1	2.6	2.4
Mean sex difference**		**3.0**	0.1	**0.8**	**1.5**	0.4	**0.4**

*Standard deviation **Differences that are statistically significant are shown in bold*

Relationship of scores between checklists

Table 18 shows the correlations between the Student, Teacher and Parent Checklists based on the overall emotional literacy scores. The checklists are moderately correlated and are statistically significant.

Table 18: Correlations between the checklists based on overall emotional literacy scores

	Student Checklist	Teacher Checklist	Parent Checklist
Student Checklist	1.00	0.28	0.38
Teacher Checklist	0.28	1.00	0.43
Parent Checklist	0.38	0.43	1.00

References

Bar-On, R. (1997) *Bar-On Emotional Quotient Inventory: Technical Manual*. Toronto: Multi-Health Systems.

Blagg, N., Ballinger, M., Garoner, R., Petty, M. & Williams, G. (1988) *Somerset Thinking Skills Course*. Oxford: Blackwell.

Breakwell, G.M. (1997) *Coping with Aggressive Behaviour*. Leicester: British Psychological Society.

Brett, D. (1988) *Annie Stories*. New York: Workman Publishing.

Brett, D. (1992) *More Annie Stories: Therapeutic Storytelling Techniques*. New York: Magination Press.

Buzan, T. (1993) *The Mind Map Book*. London: BBC Books.

Canter, L. & Canter, M. (1997) *Assertive Discipline: Positive Behavior Management for Today's Classroom*. Santa Monica, CA: Lee Canter & Assoc.

Committee for Children (1999) *Second Step: A Violence Prevention Curriculum*. Seattle, WA: Committee for Children.

Cooper, R.K. & Sawaf, A. (1995) *The EQ Map*. New York: Berkley Publishing Group.

DfES (1998) *Healthy Schools – National Healthy Schools Standard Guide*. Nottingham: DfES Publications.

Dodge, K. (1999) Taxonomy of Problematic Social Situations (TOPS) in Frederickson, N. & Cameron, R.J. (eds) *Psychology in Education Portfolio*. London: nferNelson.

Dulewicz, V. & Higgs, M. (1999) *Emotional Intelligence Questionnaire*. London: nferNelson.

Dweck, C.S. (1999) *Self-Theories: Their Role in Motivation, Personality and Development*. Philadelphia, PA: Psychology Press.

Education Act (1997) *Chapter 44: School Discipline*. London: HMSO.

Faupel, A., Herrick, E. & Sharp, P. (1998) *Anger Management: A Practical Guide*. London: David Fulton.

Feindler, E.L. & Ecton, R.B. (1986) *Adolescent Anger Control: Cognitive Behavioral Techniques*. New York: Pergamon.

Fraser, B.J. (1990) *Individualised Classroom Environment Questionnaire*. Melbourne, Australia: Australian Council for Educational Research.

Goleman, D. (1996) *Emotional Intelligence. Why It Can Matter More Than IQ*. London: Bloomsbury.

Greenberg, M.T., Kusch, C.A., Cook, E.T. & Quamma, J.P. (1995) Promoting Emotional Competence in School-Aged Children: The Effects of the PATHS Curriculum. *Development & Psychopathology*, 7: 117–36.

Jolly, M. & McNamara, E. (undated) The Behaviour Survey Checklist. In *Towards Better Behaviour*. Merseyside: PBM (7 Quinton Close, Ainsdale, Merseyside PR8 2TD).

Lewin, K. (1966) *Principles of Topological Psychology*. New York: McGraw-Hill (first published in 1936).

Mosely, J. & Tew, M. (1999) *Quality Circle Time in the Secondary School: A Handbook of Good Practice*. London: David Fulton.

Qualifications & Curriculum Authority (2002) *Citizenship at Key Stages 1 and 2*. London: QCA.

Sharp, P. (2001) *Nurturing Emotional Literacy: A Practical Guide for Teachers, Parents and Those in the Caring Professions*. London: David Fulton.

Steiner, C. with Perry, P. (1997) *Achieving Emotional Literacy: A Personal Program to Increase your Emotional Intelligence*. New York: Avon.

Wainwright, G.R. (1993) *Teach Yourself Body Language*. Sevenoaks: Hodder & Stoughton.

Bibliography and resources

Apter, T. (1997) *The Confident Child: Emotional Coaching for the Crucial Decade – Ages Five to Fifteen*. New York: Norton.
  An interesting but difficult read for parents.

Bar-On, R. & Parker, J. (2000) *The Handbook of Emotional Intelligence: Theory, Development, Assessment and Application at Home, School and in the Workplace*. California: Jossey-Bass.
  Reuven Bar-On has been a pioneer in the area of emotional literacy. His *EQi* is probably the most widely used and researched instrument in the world of work.

Ciarrochi, J., Forgas, J. & Mayer, J. (2001) *Emotional Intelligence in Everyday Life*. Philadelphia: Psychology Press.
  This is a good introduction to the topic from an academic point of view, with a very useful chapter by Maurice Elias on emotional literacy and education.

Faupel, A., Herrick, E. & Sharp, P. (1998) *Anger Management: A Practical Guide for Teachers and Parents*. London: David Fulton.
  'Very user-friendly guide which has much to offer those coming new to anger management, as well as some novel approaches' (*Young Minds Review*, 1998)

Goleman, D. (1996) *Emotional Intelligence. Why It Can Matter More Than IQ*. London: Bloomsbury.
  The world best-seller that crossed over from business to education to parenting. Holds the basic view that excellence is more than IQ and that emotional intelligence is at least as important as IQ.

Goleman, D. (1999) *Working with Emotional Intelligence*. London: Bloomsbury.
  The sequel to *Emotional Intelligence*, this book applies to organisations or institutions.

Goleman, D. (2003) *Destructive Emotions: A Scientific Dialogue with the Dalai Lama*. New York: Bantam.
  A fascinating account of a debate about destructive emotions with implications for school-based interventions, increasing self-awareness, managing anger and becoming more empathic.

Greenhalgh, P. (1994) *Emotional Growth and Learning*. London: Routledge.
  Covers how to provide emotional security for vulnerable pupils, curriculum, organisations. Well worth reading.

LeDoux, J. (1998) *The Emotional Brain*. London: Phoenix.
  The most accessible account of recent findings in neuropsychology.

National Emotional Literacy Interest Group www.nelig.com

Salovey, P. & Sluyter, D.J. (1997) *Emotional Development and Emotional Intelligence: Educational Implications*. New York: Basic Books.
  This is the classic academic text providing a comprehensive exploration of emotional literacy.

Segal, J. (1997) *Raising your Emotional Intelligence – A Practical Guide.* New York: Owl Books, Henry Holt and Company.

> Feeling smart, living smart, staying smart: the ten-step curriculum for emotional wisdom. A programme for harnessing the power of your instincts and emotions.

Stein, S. & Book, H. (2001) *The EQ Edge: Emotional Intelligence and Your Success.* London: Kogan Page.

> Based on the data provided by the Bar-On *EQi*, this book is very useful for exploring the main dimensions of emotional literacy.

Steiner, C. with Perry, P. (1997) *Achieving Emotional Literacy: A Personal Program to Increase your Emotional Intelligence.* New York: Avon.

> The authors are psychologists with a long track record of clinical work and publications. Start with yourself before helping others to develop emotional literacy.

Weisinger, H. (1997) *Managing Emotional Intelligence at Work.* California: Jossey-Bass.

> Covers EQ, emotions, motivation, communication and helping others to help themselves.

Wycoff, J. (1991) *Mindmapping: Your Personal Guide to Exploring Creativity and Problem-Solving.* New York: Berkley Books.

> A clear introduction to the use and applications of the mind-mapping technique, illustrated with easy-to-follow examples.

All the published games described in this Guide can be obtained from Smallwood Publishing Ltd. This is a publisher and mail order supplier of innovative resources for mental health professionals and educators. A subsidiary, 'Being Yourself', offers materials for direct work with children. In addition to books, 'Being Yourself' stocks therapeutic games and therapist's puppets.

Smallwood Publishing Ltd
The Old Bakery
Charlton House
Dour Street
DOVER
Kent CT16 1ED, UK

Phone & Fax: ++44 (0)1304 226900
Website: www.smallwood.co.uk

Interventions

Disclaimer: The interventions and activities presented here are used by the emotional literacy support services in Southampton and have been adapted for use in this Guide. To the best of our knowledge, these activities have not been published elsewhere and we have made acknowledgements to published material where appropriate.

● 46   Emotional Literacy: Assessment and Intervention – Ages 11 to 16 **USER'S GUIDE**

Introduction

To be meaningful, assessment should lead to action to change an existing situation. This section of the Guide outlines a selection of things that can be done in the case of emotional literacy (see also Frameworks 1 and 2, pages 18 and 20).

- Some of these interventions or activities are concerned with changing what the school or teacher does in order to make the environment in which students are functioning more conducive to the acquisition and maintenance of emotional literacy skills – **environmental changes**.
- Some of the interventions focus on ways in which others respond to appropriate and inappropriate behaviours – **consequences**.
- Finally, students themselves may need to learn individual skills and competences and these can be taught directly – **teaching personal competences**.

This threefold focus – on the environment, on consequences or responses, and on teaching individual skills and competences – reflects a concern to uphold the general principle that emotional and social behaviour is a function of the interaction between the context and what the individual brings into that context. It also helps to avoid deficit models in which the student is pathologised or blamed. The latter can so easily be perceived by students as judgemental and this is a fundamental threat to their sense of self-worth. This perceived threat can produce the strong emotional reactions of anger and anxiety, and hence anti-social behaviour.

When thinking about behaviours to replace inappropriate ones, it is important to:

1. Consider the context or environment and examine what changes could be made to make the desired behaviour more likely to occur.

2. Think about the needs that the problem behaviour is trying to meet. Ask yourself the question: 'Why, for what purpose?'. If the first answer is not in the form of a legitimate need, ask the question again until a legitimate need is established. Teach more acceptable ways to meet this legitimate need.

3. Check that the student knows *what* to do – the 'rules of the game' (for example, how to join a group conversation).

4. Check that the student has been shown *how* to do this – demonstration by adults or peers, role-play, drama, etc. – and has been given the opportunity to practise the skill through role-play, simulations, etc.

5. If all the above have been demonstrated, think about how the student could be motivated to carry out these known skills by considering rewards for doing the skill or approximations of the skill, or sanctions for not doing so.

For easy reference, the interventions have been divided into five sections, each of which relates to the dimensions of emotional literacy covered by the checklists – however, there is naturally an overlap. In addition, several techniques have wide application throughout the interventions and for emotional literacy generally, and so they are described briefly next. As the age range for whom these materials are intended is quite wide, they need to be adapted as appropriate for the student(s).

General techniques

1. The use of stories

Students who are emotionally very vulnerable perceive their world to be threatening to their core sense of belonging and worth. Because it is the *perception* and not necessarily the existence of real threat that is crucial, a change in the way the student sees the world often becomes the main focus of the intervention.

Teaching different ways of perceiving things, and teaching different beliefs and attitudes, is much more subtle and difficult than teaching new behaviours. The latter can be overtly demonstrated and role-played and feedback can be given to observed behaviour when the new skills are practised. It is much more difficult to model and demonstrate different ways of believing and thinking as these are internal psychological processes. To some extent this can be done by adults quite consciously expressing in words how they are thinking about a particular issue but, in general, the most effective way of modelling alternative and different ways of construing reality is through the use of age-appropriate stories. Sometimes called 'therapeutic metaphors', these stories are a particularly powerful and creative way of helping students to see, experience and learn different ways of thinking and believing.

There are several types of therapeutic stories and metaphors. Much of the readily available literature for young people can be used. Such literature can be used as part of a whole-class curriculum focus on particular emotions or can be used as part of individual programmes or interventions.

Therapeutic metaphors can also be created specifically for an individual in a real attempt to see the world from that student's point of view, to understand the source of the threat or stress, and to hypothesise how the stress might be better coped with if he or she could only perceive and think differently. Changes in beliefs, attitudes and self-talk can really make a difference.

The first step is to think about the problem which has created the need for a story that will demonstrate different ways of thinking and acting. It is important to try to appreciate the feelings a student is experiencing as he or she copes with a particular problem or situation.

The next step is to work out what essential message you want to get across – what kind of solution or resolution of the problem should the story either model or suggest to the student? Such solutions may involve acquiring new skills and competences or seeing how others can give us support and provide comfort and encouragement. Sometimes it is simply a matter of time healing. The story or metaphor should also relate to the student's own experiences or hobbies. It will contain a hero or heroine as the main character who will be like the student to some extent, perhaps having some of the strengths and competences the student has or looking like the individual or being in a similar situation. It is good practice to give the hero or heroine a name that begins with the same sound as the student's name (for example, Lisa for Lucy, Sam for Simon) as the individual needs to be able to identify at some level with the main character. Essentially the story needs to mirror the essential problem the student is experiencing and then to model different processes of thinking and behaviour and how the situation is coped with or resolved for the heroine or hero.

There are some excellent guidelines for creating such stories in Brett's *Annie Stories* and *More Annie Stories: Therapeutic Storytelling Techniques* (1988, 1992). Although written for parents with younger children, the principles outlined on composing stories are applicable to teachers and other adults working with any age group in school.

There are many advantages in writing and giving such stories to students. It is first of all important to the student that an adult has taken time and effort to create and give them something intensely personal. Such stories can be read at a variety of levels – from an unconscious level using symbolic material (as do many fairytales) to the much more pragmatic paralleling of the student's actual situation. Metaphors and allegories do not need to be interpreted: whether the student wants to talk about them or not is almost irrelevant. Stories are given to students for them to make what they like out of them.

The students can be involved at a variety of levels such as improving the story, illustrating it and wordprocessing it. Finally, the flexibility gained from the use of stories and metaphors is almost infinite: they can be used with students with very poor academic attainments and right across the age range.

EXAMPLE OF A THERAPEUTIC METAPHOR

This story was told to a 15-year-old female student. She was considered to be academically able to achieve excellent GCSE results, but was very confrontational to teachers and was truanting regularly with the apparent collusion of her parents on occasion. It might be thought that such a simple story told to a sophisticated student would be seen as childish and silly. In fact, having heard the story, the student said, 'That's me, isn't, it?'. She was then able to explore the nature of her relationships with some teachers and was able to appreciate that some teachers can react emotionally to students owing to their own anxieties and fears and became aware of her own part in maintaining confrontational relationships. The story opened up exploration of a number of personal issues, including the very ambivalent messages her mother was giving her daughter about the importance of attending school while apparently, on another level, colluding with her absences.

Catherine's long journey

Once upon a time, probably in early Medieval England, a mother and her young daughter, Catherine, were living in a poor part of town. They weren't starving, but they didn't have much and life was hard. I don't know much about their history, or how they came to be living there and why they were on their own. The mother had been told that she was, in fact, a princess but that she would only be recognised as a princess if she travelled to her own land – a very distant country. She had never managed to go to the far-distant country and, feeling that she had missed her great opportunity, she was determined that her daughter would not miss out too and should travel to their distant land. However, Catherine's mother had very mixed and ambivalent feelings – on the one hand she wanted her daughter to go but, on the other, she was scared that she would lose her. She was also a bit jealous that, if Catherine went, she would have even more regret that she herself had missed out.

The young daughter gradually grew up and the time approached when she knew that she would have to go. Catherine felt very unsure about it all – her mother was determined that she must go, but she was frightened of missing the warmth and love of her home and was fearful of the unknown. It was going to be a very long journey and the country Catherine was going to have to travel through was, she had been told, full of very unfriendly people and dangerous dragons. So she was going to have to be very brave to cope with her loneliness and fear. It was a long journey and it was going to be very monotonous and boring, trudging day after day, mile after mile, while at the same time thinking of all the exciting things she could have been doing at home.

So the time came for Catherine to set out. She really didn't want to go but she knew that it would be all right in the end if she persevered. It was a real dilemma for her, and she started her journey with a heavy heart. As she travelled to the next country, it was just as bad as everyone had warned her. The people were unfriendly and treated her badly, and she saw and heard dragons not far away.

However, a wise old man had advised Catherine before she went that, despite all her fears and anxieties, she should try to smile at the unfriendly people. As she journeyed on, trying to do this, she found that, at first, people only occasionally smiled back. But gradually they seemed to be much more friendly and she joined a group of travellers who were going to her new country too. They also told her that the dragons were really very friendly and were not at all dangerous – although when the dragons picked up people's fear of them, they could only handle their own nervousness by becoming extremely aggressive and by being fierce and threatening. Suddenly, a great weight seemed to lift off Catherine's shoulders. The journey now seemed to go really quickly and she soon reached the frontier. All of a sudden, Catherine was recognised as the princess's daughter and everyone started singing and dancing.

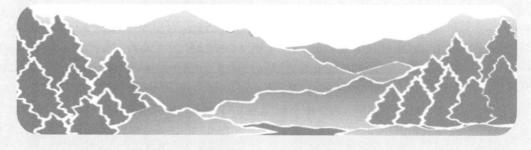

2. I-messages and you-messages

Given that the fundamental need of children and young people is to belong and to feel a sense of value and lovableness, the way they perceive adults to be treating them is fundamental to the kinds of emotions they are likely to experience. The way in which adults communicate can either help students to feel that they are of value and that they belong, or it can be perceived as a psychological axe against which they will attack (anger) or run away from (anxiety) or, in extreme circumstances, play dead (depression). Communication is made up of two major elements – verbal and non-verbal – and, although it is thought that we convey the most powerful messages non-verbally, the words we use are nevertheless still very important.

Words that convey judgement are particularly powerful emotionally. A non-judgemental communication is one in which the individual is not judged to be a bad person, rather the behaviour is seen as inappropriate and unacceptable; it distinguishes the person from his or her behaviour. A non-judgemental communication is also one that does not impute evil motives to the person: in fact, at its best, it does the opposite and conveys that the behaviour has been an attempt, however poor, to try to meet legitimate needs.

I-messages are verbal communications which, particularly when we are reproaching a student for 'bad' behaviour, still try to convey a fundamentally non-judgemental attitude. They are contrasted with you-messages which are blaming and judgemental: '*You are ...* [disobedient, thoughtless, selfish, lazy, inconsiderate]'. These global judgements do not distinguish between the person and his or her behaviour and they impute an essential badness to the person. You-messages often also contain adverbs like 'always' or 'never'.

I-messages, on the other hand, convey the effect of what the other person has done on 'me' and it is difficult to contest the truth of 'my' feelings. So I-messages describe how 'I' am feeling and then describe the behaviour that has led to these feelings: '*I feel* ... [disappointed, let down, put upon, or annoyed] when you forget to do your homework'. The message can be de-personalised even further by substituting 'students' for 'you': '*I feel* let down when *students* don't keep the rules about running in the corridor that we have all agreed'.

I-messages are thought to be much better when we are praising students also. Dweck's work (1999) suggests that praise which is directed to the behaviour rather than to the inherent qualities of the student leads to more persistence in the face of difficulty or challenge: 'I am very pleased that you have used your checklist for remembering how to tackle this work'.

I-messages do not come easily – they need to be consciously practised until they become part of the teacher's spontaneous repertoire, particularly in the face of inappropriate behaviour.

3. The use of games

Many of our personal skills and competences in the area of emotional literacy can be learned and, more especially, practised in the context of games. A number of games, that combine elements of imagination, competition and fun, have been devised for use in teaching emotional literacy skills and competences.

Several of these games are used in anger management, social skills and self-esteem groups or individually with an adult, but it is probably the modification and further development of the ideas in these games (both published and in 'folklore') that is the hallmark of effective work with people experiencing difficulties. Rather like therapeutic stories, such games can be tailor-made to the needs of individuals. They provide a safe and sometimes highly structured environment to raise very personal issues, to allow the consideration of other perspectives and alternative ways of seeing the world or particular problems and enable the sharing of other students' experiences. Games often provide opportunities for rehearsing strategies both mentally and sometimes physically in various forms of role-play. (The use of puppets has proved useful for many 11- and 12-year-olds, allowing them space to communicate and reflect upon aspects of their experience which otherwise would not have been accessible to them.)

The adults together with the students need to establish clear ground rules for any games, especially ensuring that there is freedom for students to opt out at any time.

Some of the published games found to be particularly useful in the field of emotional literacy can be bought from Smallwood Publishing (see page 44) and include:

- *The Mad, Sad, Glad Game* produced by Peak Potential Inc., Loveland, Connecticut, USA – this game looks at empathy, labelling feelings, anger, bullying issues, and helping to express feelings about difficult situations in words or non-verbally.
- *The Talking, Feeling and Doing Game* by Richard Gardner at Creative Therapeutics Inc. Creskill, New Jersey 07626 – this board game is designed to help people talk about their emotional reactions to situations, especially those who find it difficult to 'open up' and communicate their feelings.
- *The Ungame* from Talicor Games – this non-competitive game is useful as an icebreaker activity for a group leading to a serious exchange of thoughts and feelings.
- *The Conflict Resolution Game* from the Center for Applied Psychology, King of Prussia, PA, USA – a board game suitable for the first few years of secondary school, designed to teach solving conflicts peaceably.
- *The Anger Solution Game* from the Center for Applied Psychology, King of Prussia, PA, USA – this game enables students to effectively identify, express and manage anger.
- *All About Me* produced by Barnardo's – this board game facilitates communication and sheltered self-disclosure about oneself, one's attitudes, emotions, etc.

4. Behavioural contracts

Even when it can be demonstrated that a student possesses the required skills and competences for a particular behaviour, they may not use the behaviour because they do not want to. Behavioural contracts can be used to tackle this situation as they focus on the motivational aspects of carrying out more appropriate behaviour. Of course, they are not contracts in any legal sense and need to be distinguished from home-school contracts that have featured in recent legislation.

Behavioural contracts provide a structured way for adults within the school to *negotiate* a way for a student to change his or her behaviour. Contracts that do not involve the student but are simply imposed by adults are often found to be ineffective.

The following guidelines need to be followed for contracts to be effective:

1. The problem needs to be clearly identified and described and patterns of intensity, duration and frequency explored to highlight particular situations for the contract to deal with.

2. There needs to be a fairly informal discussion with someone who has the confidence of the student in which background difficulties and the possibility of using rewards to help change the behaviour are explored. Identifying what might be rewarding to the student is very important at this point. Often these rewards will be at home rather than at school and, if this is the case, the issue needs to be informally discussed with the parents.

3. Negotiation follows with the various parties – student, parents and school – to draw up an agreement that, if the student uses an agreed behaviour, the parents and school agree to do or give the 'reward'. This needs to be expressed very clearly in words that describe precisely who will do what and when. The form of words used should not set 'fuzzy' unclear targets such as 'Gita will behave well during maths lessons', but should be precise such as 'Gita will not talk to other students, unless given explicit permission to do otherwise, during maths lessons'.

4. There should be a clear starting point and end point, with agreed dates on which the 'contract' will be reviewed. It is often useful to have a 'mediator' who is not directly involved – someone from outside the school, such as an educational psychologist, education welfare officer or a behaviour support worker.

5. A good behavioural contract should have the headings and content listed below:
   - names of people involved – student, sometimes peers, parents, school staff, mediator, etc.;
   - when the contract will begin and end;
   - description of specific targets or behaviours (and these will include not only what the student agrees to do, but also what the school and parents will do);
   - how data will be collected and how the contract will be monitored to ensure that all parties are carrying out the agreement;
   - consequences or rewards for carrying out the behaviours agreed;
   - a bonus clause – something extra that will happen if performance exceeds that described in the target;
   - a penalty clause – if thought desirable, this will describe sanctions for not complying with the agreement;
   - what will happen if there is a dispute about the running of the agreement;
   - signatures of all the parties involved.

5. Feelings vocabulary

The feelings vocabulary list found in **Worksheet 1** may be useful in many of the activities. While not comprehensive, it simply provides alternative emotion words to increase the students' vocabulary. Appropriate age-level words can be selected from the list and used in the activities that require the use of feelings vocabulary.

Developing self-awareness

The skills and competences of this dimension relate to the students' ability to be able to recognise, label and understand their own emotions.

Self-awareness consists of a group of skills and competences that are very important in emotional literacy, and they are probably the foundation on which all the others depend. Interpersonal and social situations provide us with tasks to achieve every day – how to initiate a relationship, how to repair a situation that has led to anger, how to cope with failure or teasing, how to handle winning so that we do not put somebody else down.

If we are not aware of our own feelings, if we are unable to label them and discriminate between them, we will not be aware of other people's feelings either – this awareness constitutes the basis of empathy. It is also unlikely that we will know the appropriate behaviours with which to preserve our own self-worth and that of other people as well. Such behaviours are the social skills for everyday living.

This section therefore provides a number of activities that are designed to help students to be able to label, discriminate between, and understand their own emotions.

Gets upset easily or complains

Students sometimes display emotions in an exaggerated way when the circumstances, or triggers, would not usually warrant this. The student is considered to be 'hypersensitive' to emotional issues.

Environmental changes

▶ **Understanding the function of the behaviour**

The first task of the adult is to try to understand how this emotional response is helping the student to preserve his or her sense of self-esteem. Questions to ask are:

- What issues are provoking this emotional over-reaction?
- Is the student being 'attacked' by bullying or by threat of rejection and abandonment in friendship issues?
- Is the student unable to express emotions in a 'graduated' way, so that it is only by expressing emotions in an extreme way that he or she feels noticed?
- Is the student's vulnerability due to family issues, especially marital breakdown, bereavement (including pets, losing or falling out with a special friend), moving house, etc.?
- Are there issues within the school such as the threat to self-esteem of tests/examinations, changes in routines or teachers, or in academic tasks becoming more demanding?
- Is this hypersensitivity to emotional issues a new pattern?
- Is the behaviour learned behaviour and reinforced by peers, parents or teachers?

- Is there any pattern in where, when and with whom the student appears more vulnerable to upset? Can you spot the triggers?
- As physical factors can affect our hypersensitivity and emotional reactions, are there issues of physical health, puberty, hunger, thirst, poor sleeping patterns, etc.?
- Are there any changes in physical appearance that can lead to becoming hyper-sensitive about self-image – is the student becoming overweight, recently wearing glasses or teeth braces, etc.?

▶ **Changing the response/empathy**

Try to change your response from simply sympathy to communicating that you recognise the student is feeling sad, unhappy or distressed. You can also talk about what you or the student could do to help with these overpowering feelings.

Try to notice when the student appears down, sad or unhappy, and attempt to change the general atmosphere in the class, perhaps by one of the following methods.

▶ **Circle time**

Circle time provides a good forum to discuss feelings and reactions. Use a round of *'I get upset and I am unhappy when ... and I help myself feel happy again by ...'* to talk about feelings, to discover triggers for individuals and to allow students to hear alternative strategies from their peers.

▶ **Buddies**

The use of 'buddies' is helpful. The teacher works with understanding and empathic students, supporting them in consciously being a friend and companion to another student during breaktime or with difficult work.

▶ **Distraction techniques**

Distract the student when you notice 'sensitive' issues arising, perhaps by giving him or her a task: *'Please take a message to ...'* or changing the focus of the current activity.

▶ **Personal space**

Introduce a system (for example, cards showing symbols of different emotions) by which a student is given or can request some personal space away from the 'pressures'.

Consequences

◼ Reinforcement

Try to ensure that you are rewarding the types of response you would like to see by noticing the appropriate response and praising the student. Notice when students are not hypersensitive in situations where they might normally be so and specifically praise and describe their efforts.

Teaching personal competences

● Interpretation of events

Hypersensitivity or emotional over-reaction is related to how the student perceives his or her 'world'. If students could perceive this as not being so threatening to their sense of self-worth, their emotional reaction would be different. Such students need to see the world more 'realistically' and to understand that their worth and dignity does not depend upon what happens to them. Teaching these students that the way they interpret events affects how they feel, and describing or demonstrating how other people learn to cope with strong feelings, can be worked on using stories and therapeutic metaphors (see page 48 for further information on the use of stories). It may be helpful to discuss **Worksheet 2** and to work through a student's responses to the questions presented there about what made him/her upset and what s/he was thinking at the time.

● One-to-one counselling methods

In one-to-one counselling situations, students can use drawings and poetry to describe the kinds of things that make them upset and how they might cope with these feelings. The student can be asked to draw pictures of situations in which they feel upset or to help create stories about how people who feel very sad can cope with the situation. They could also be asked what they might suggest to their best friend who is very sad to help him or her feel better – what might they do or say to themselves, who they might talk to, etc.

● Setting targets

Use quite specific targets for the students to achieve (for example, not getting upset or complaining during the morning when things go wrong) and reward this achievement. A simple, informal behavioural contract might be appropriate in some circumstances (see page 52 for further information on the use of behavioural contracts).

● Finds it difficult to accept constructive criticism and feedback

One of the key skills of self-awareness is to recognise our own strengths and weaknesses. We form a more realistic view of ourselves by being open both to praise when we have achieved something positive and to constructive criticism when our performance is somehow lacking. This is particularly true in the school situation where feedback is crucial to academic learning.

Some students, however, react emotionally to feedback about their work and behaviour. Such emotional reactions are fundamentally due to the student interpreting correction, marking or criticism as a personal attack on their self-worth and responding to such a threat either by becoming angry or aggressive or by withdrawing by running away or crying, or simply giving up.

Environmental changes

Adults should consider what they might do to lessen students' *perception* of criticism being an attack on their self-worth.

▶ **Style of feedback**

Students differ in the way they respond to particular forms of criticism. An emotional reaction is more likely if their work is returned with corrections (especially if there are a large number), without accompanying verbal explanation and support and encouragement. It is good practice, particularly with the student who handles criticism badly, to give verbal feedback in private first and then to provide some written comments as a more permanent record. The teacher needs to be sensitive to the student's emotional state when feedback is being given, particularly emphasising the positives and choosing only one or two aspects for improvement. It is always important to focus on effort rather than attainment and on improvement over previous attempts rather than on absolute standards.

▶ **Focus on the behaviour not the person**

Make sure that issues are depersonalised, focusing on the behaviour and not the person and using I-messages rather than you-messages (see page 51 for further information).

▶ **Feedback forms**

The use of a standard 'honest' feedback form such as the one shown in **Worksheet 3** takes the person out of the firing line and focuses both on positives and on something the student can work on.

▶ **Self-evaluation**

Self-evaluation rather than teacher evaluation can be beneficial. For this, teachers help students to set realistic goals and then, when the work is complete, encourage them to consider and write down three good things about what they have done and one thing they might be able to improve.

Consequences

■ **How to criticise**

It is important to recognise that students differ in their reactions to public praise and public criticism. Even the general rule of 'praise in public, criticise in private' needs to be carefully considered. Certainly, wherever possible, criticise in private but some students may also become embarrassed by public praise and the teacher needs to be sensitive to this. (See also the information on I-messages and you-messages on page 51, relating to criticising the behaviour rather than the student.)

Behavioural contracts

With those students who find constructive feedback difficult to accept, the teacher needs to be sensitive to times when they have accepted such criticism appropriately. This behaviour needs to be rewarded and specifically described. Arising out of one-to-one work, specific targets for accepting criticism can be set if this is a major problem and some kind of informal contract drawn up (see page 52 for further information on the use of contracts).

Teaching personal competences

Adopting alternative strategies

Different and alternative ways of viewing feedback and constructive criticism need to be taught to the student. The student is reacting emotionally because such criticism is being perceived as an attack. Alternative strategies could be explored during whole-class interventions such as circle time – students could consider questions like: *'How do I feel when …?'* and *'How can I improve …?'*.

Adopting alternative thinking

Emotional reactions to feedback are usually due to students being unable to accept that, in the same way that we are all complex individuals with 'good' and 'bad' characteristics, our work will also have good and bad points. What needs to be changed is the 'all-or-nothing' and 'black-and-white' thinking. In addition, it is better to regard work as having 'strengths and weaknesses' rather than 'good and bad' points. Thus, when students show very strong and unhelpful emotions towards criticisms of their work, they need to be able to view all their work as having strengths and weaknesses rather than being a good or bad piece of work.

Activities with individuals and small groups to try to move students away from all-or-nothing thinking towards a more realistic view of strengths and weaknesses could involve listing the characteristics of a 'celebrity' across a range of situations (appearance, work, family life, attitudes and values, etc.). The reality that emerges is always a combination of strengths and weaknesses.

Stories

It is helpful to construct stories or to use published stories that demonstrate the way different people react to criticism and the consequences of these different reactions in how people feel and then behave (see page 48 for information on the use of stories).

Seems unable to recognise the early signs of becoming angry

Self-awareness relates to self-regulation in the sense that, if students tend to be unaware of what is happening to them emotionally, they will be unable to exercise control over their emotions. This is particularly true in the case of anger: if the early signs of frustration like irritation and annoyance are not picked up, anger is likely to be then experienced as overwhelming.

Environmental changes

▶ **Teaching about emotions**

The reasons why people become angry and the types of triggers that often lead to anger could form part of the taught curriculum. The 'Firework Model' (Feindler & Ecton, 1986; Faupel *et al.*, 1998) is particularly useful in helping students understand the functions of anger and the kinds of triggers that tend to provoke anger. For a firework to explode, three things are necessary. The 'match' represents the event that sparks off the outburst (that is, what somebody does – for example, calling the student a name). The 'fuse' stands for the thoughts and interpretations that the student puts on the event. (For example, the same remark made by a best friend might be interpreted very differently.) The 'dynamite or explosive' represents the person's aroused state. If the 'dynamite' is damp, the firework will not be ignited properly – the student gets into a physiologically non-aroused state, for example by slowing down the rate of breathing to about six breaths per minute.

The curriculum should explicitly deal with the physiological changes that we notice as we become more and more emotional. The body is preparing itself either to fight or to flee, both of which demand strenuous exertion. These physiological changes include faster and shallower breathing to obtain the oxygen necessary to enable the release of energy by burning glucose which is stored in the muscles. The heart beats faster, to take the oxygen in the blood quickly to the muscles. 'Butterflies' in the stomach and uncomfortable knotted feelings in the stomach occur when the blood moves from the digestive system to the muscles. This movement of the blood to the muscles also accounts for the person becoming 'white with anger'. The fact that we tend to perspire and sweat is the body's way of providing a cooling mechanism by using evaporation. The tense, fidgety knees-knocking feelings are the muscles getting ready to spring into action, rather like a cat twitches just before it springs.

▶ **Identifying emotions**

Teachers can model the processes by which they read how students are feeling. For example, you may notice changes in their breathing patterns, facial expressions, clenched fists and other body postures and can express this openly: *'I can see that you might be feeling cross, because I notice ... '.*

The physiological and behavioural signs of various emotions can be illustrated and explored using drama and role-play focusing on body language – for example, in how people start to show they are angry.

Students could be asked to produce a video to show facial expressions in different emotions or use computer graphics to demonstrate how different parts of the face appear in different emotions.

▶ **Recognising emotions (1)**

The teacher can set up a system to communicate to an individual when he or she notices the first signs of the student becoming angry. It could be a card or some gesture explained previously to the student.

Consequences

■ **Praise**

As the main aim is to help the student begin to demonstrate awareness of the early stages of becoming angry, rewards and praise need to be built in by the teacher when the student first demonstrates this early awareness. There should be rewards and praise for the student when he or she responds to the system that has been set up to help achieve awareness (see 'Recognising emotions (1)' on page 60).

Teaching personal competences

● **Recognising emotions (2)**

Work with an individual student can develop and extend the environmental interventions outlined above. For example, the system set up for the teacher to convey when he or she first notices the student becoming angry can move to the next step whereby the students have a system for showing the teacher that they have noticed themselves becoming angry or upset.

● **Using a mirror**

A mirror can be used to help the student try to express different emotional states, particularly irritation, annoyance, frustration and anger. These expressions can be modelled by adults or peers.

● **Recording emotions**

A framework for identifying and recording on a daily basis the kinds of situations or triggers that spark off anger can be developed. This could be done by adapting a 'feelings graph' (see **Worksheet 5**) to plot levels of anger throughout the day and answering the questions from **Worksheet 4**: *'What happened? What was I thinking/feeling? What happened next?'*.

● **Generating alternative interpretations**

Help students to identify what kind of things they are saying to themselves when they start to become angry. These usually attribute hostile or aggressive intentions to peers or adults towards themselves. Getting them to generate other possible interpretations can be helpful. Using or adapting **Worksheet 2** can be helpful in generating alternative ways of thinking about a situation.

● Cannot identify different emotions or label own feelings

This is one of the most important skills for any growth in emotional literacy. Without the language to describe and identify different emotional states, young people cannot learn to regulate and handle situations of threat to their feelings of belonging and self-worth.

Environmental changes

▶ **Emotion of the week**

A whole-school curriculum that focuses on the variety of different emotions is a useful approach. An emotion of the week, month or half-term can be appointed which becomes the focus of assembly, displays and collages in art, classwork in English, and role-playing to guess the feeling in drama. Such a curriculum enables students to identify and discriminate among different emotions, giving students a vocabulary to describe how they and other people are feeling. With the increasing age and maturity of students, the range of emotions and discrimination between emotions will become increasingly sophisticated. The curriculum materials used will therefore need to keep in step with the ability of the students.

▶ **Circle time**

Use circle time to explore how students are currently feeling and when and where they experience named emotions. It is helpful for students to see how others are feeling and how they deal with these feelings.

▶ **Feelings dictionary/database**

Develop a class feelings dictionary, illustrated by drawings, photographs, magazine pictures, etc. Alternatively, a class computer database of different emotions could be established and built-up over the course of the year.

▶ **I-messages**

Teachers can model how they themselves are feeling using a wide variety of emotional labels. I-messages are an effective way of doing this: '*I feel* ... [irritated, angry, disappointed, ill-at-ease, put-upon] ... *when people* ...' (see page 51 for further information).

Consequences

■ **Labelling emotions**

Notice and praise the use of a variety of appropriate labels for different emotions. For example, praise and reward students for completing their feelings diaries (see page 63). Reinforce the use of methods and techniques for identifying and labelling emotional states by working with individuals or in small groups.

Teaching personal competences

● **Using emotion words**

Students need to develop a wide range of emotion words. They can illustrate or demonstrate these. Collect pictures showing a variety of emotional situations from magazine and newspaper pictures and help the students to use a wide range of emotion labels to describe these situations.

● **Feelings indicators**

Students can keep a feelings diary or a feelings graph whereby they attempt to review their day. Use a 'feelings wheel' (page 98) or a 'feelings scale' when asking students to rate how they themselves felt about a particular activity and to provide descriptive labels. Several of the possible whole-class curriculum interventions (such as 'Emotion of the week', page 62, 'Feelings diaries', teaching students themselves to use I-messages, page 51, and so on) can be developed or extended in individual or small group sessions. Two of these methods are described below.

● **Feelings diaries**

Students can be asked to keep feelings diaries. An example is presented in **Worksheet 4**. Students can be asked to draw in their own personalised representations of the emotions listed if preferred. Simply photocopy **Worksheet 4** and erase the drawings. Computerised diaries can be compiled, if preferred. Feelings diaries are designed to help students identify and label their feelings, but also to give them an understanding of the relationship between how they feel at any one moment and the context and triggers which 'provoke' that emotion. This can help students to think about ways they could control their negative feelings by avoiding these triggers where possible, but also by changing the way they think about them in the first place.

● **Feelings graphs**

The feelings graph in **Worksheet 5** can be photocopied and completed by the students. This type of graph is usually used in individual counselling sessions but can be used in a class setting also. The student is asked to review a period of time, usually a week or day (if using the time period of a day, photocopy the worksheet and then replace the days of the week with timings or events). Annotations are made on the graph by the student. For example, the first event might be 'waking up' and the student is asked to mark a cross on the graph to indicate how happy (use positive wording) he or she was feeling at that time. The next events might be 'catching the bus' and 'arriving at school', and so on. The crosses on the graph are then joined up to give a visual representation of the student's mood throughout the day. This can be used in a variety of ways to explore perceptions, possibilities of changes and even as a pre- and post-intervention tool.

Is unaware of own strengths and weaknesses

This addresses two possible scenarios:

● students who have an inflated and unrealistic view of their skills and competences and are unaware of weaknesses;
● students who think that they are incompetent when in fact they have considerable ability and are therefore unaware of their strengths.

Of course, there are students who have inflated views about some aspects of themselves while believing themselves to be useless in other areas. An example of the latter might be a student who sees himself as incompetent in academic learning but who, with no obvious special talent, sees himself as a professional footballer with the local premiership club. Emotionally literate views of oneself are neither wildly exaggerated nor so low as to produce helplessness and unwillingness to even try.

Environmental changes

The teacher's knowledge and understanding of his or her individual students is key to helping students achieve realistic views of themselves.

For students who have exaggerated views of their abilities, carefully crafted specific comments emphasising the need to work on improvement areas will convey a more realistic view of their abilities without destroying what is in effect a very fragile self-esteem. In fact, exaggerated views of themselves are usually a tactic to defend poor self-image. Rather than confronting their inflated views directly, it is preferable to build up general self-esteem first. If this is achieved, the expression of inflated skills and abilities gradually tends to recede because if students feel good about themselves they are not so hypersensitive to attacks on their self-worth. The lower the sense of self-worth, the more we need to keep scanning the social and interpersonal horizon for threat.

▶ **Points systems**

The use of merits, points and certificates are useful ways of communicating success and approval. But they carry with them some dangers, most of which can be avoided if students are set individual targets towards which they are working and rewards are given dependent upon the effort being expended in reaching them. The way these are visually presented needs to avoid the not uncommon sight of model students with lines of merits and points and other students standing out as achieving nothing. Teachers and schools need to carefully monitor the distribution of merits, certificates and prizes to ensure that all students have equal access to them.

The content for which praise and recognition is given needs to be conceived as broadly as possible so that it includes not only academic, but practical and other skills and, very importantly, the social and interpersonal achievements of being helpful, co-operative and handling stress, etc.

▶ **Matching tasks to ability**

Students who are unaware of their own strengths play down their ability and often first respond to challenges with *'I can't'* and frequently then do not even attempt the task. There needs to be a careful match between the ability of individual students and the task they are being asked to tackle. It is important to involve students in identifying what aspects of the work they can do, which bits might be difficult for them and how they can cope with these difficulties, followed up by self-rating or evaluation after the task is completed. (**Worksheet 13** might be useful in this context.)

▶ **Student of the week**

For younger students, another whole-class strategy might be a 'student of the week box'. Each week a different student is named in turn and, during the week, the rest of the class each write down a strength or good quality of the named person and post it in the box. The box is presented to the named student at the end of the week to read the contents. This strategy may be most appropriate when used in tutor groups.

▶ **Identifying strengths**

In circle time, students identify their own strengths or the good qualities of another student. **Worksheet 6**, 'Celebrate your success', can be photocopied and used in a variety of ways to help students identify their strengths and to realise what they have achieved.

Consequences

■ **Praise effort**

The way the teacher gives praise is crucial to building up more realistic self-views. Praise needs to be sincere and genuine, it needs to be about effort and it needs to be personal in the sense that it compares the student's current performance with his or her own previous performances rather than comparing it with other students. Personal and individual targets should be set and praise given for the effort put in to achieve these rather than the use of rank ordering (who has done best and next best, etc.). This should be avoided precisely because it leads to comparisons and undermines motivation and feelings of self-worth in vulnerable students. Self-worth is built upon challenges to *'improve upon what I have been able to do previously'*.

Teaching personal competences

● **Quality log**

When working with students who continually put themselves down as 'useless', it is not usually sufficient or helpful to shower them with praise because they often do not believe that it is genuine. So a much more effective method is to attempt to get them to express and notice positive things about themselves. A 'Quality log' can be provided for the students to write about something that they have done well. Similarly, they can keep a diary in which they write down some strength or quality they have shown over the course of the day. **Worksheet 7**, the 'Quality log', can be photocopied if desired.

● **Emotional literacy checklists**

The emotional literacy checklists supplied with this Guide can be used in a positive way if students have rated themselves rather poorly on the Student Checklist. The Teacher and Parent Checklists can be used in counselling sessions to present a more realistic picture of strengths and weaknesses.

● **Challenging black-and-white thinking**

Students who consider themselves to have no good qualities are characterised by black-and-white thinking where all is good or all is bad. This 'dysfunctional thinking' leads to negative emotions. It can be tackled by empirically testing out whether black-and-white thinking is useful or true. Frequently such students say things like *'I never get anything right'* and this can be jointly tested by an adult and the student concerned by examining the student's work and showing that there are many occasions where this statement can be proved false.

● **Questioning**

In working with individual students and reviewing how the day or week has gone, it is important to ask open questions which assume that there has been something that has gone well – for example, an open question such as: *'Tell me about something that you have been pleased about today …'*.

● **Stories**

It is helpful to use stories about people with low self-esteem, showing how these story characters often completely misjudge what others think about them and how other people actually like and value them. For guidelines about compiling and using such stories see page 48.

● Worries about inadequacies and shortcomings

Students who are highly anxious perceive the world as threatening and the future as unpredictable, and see themselves as not having the resources to cope with the current threat or future unpredictability. In general terms, the task of the teacher is to reduce as far as possible the perception of the classroom as threatening and to increase its predictability. The skills and competences to be developed will revolve around changing the way students understand the significance of their own shortcomings and developing coping strategies to reduce feelings of anxiety.

Environmental changes

In what ways are classrooms likely to be threatening places? The main sources of threat essentially revolve around *judgement*, namely whether students feel they will be exposed to judgement about their own competences and skills and ultimately about their own worth. A classroom environment which is 'judgemental' is one where the teacher picks up on failure rather than success, encourages competition rather than co-operation, exposes how badly students have done or behaved rather than how well, and sets up situations or tests where students are measured against absolute standards rather than against their own previous performance.

▶ Entity versus incremental views of intelligence

A school or classroom should strongly avoid teaching the false assumption that a person's worth and value depends on how well they do or what they achieve. Some schools also tend to believe in an entity theory of intelligence, namely that intelligence is something fixed and immutable, rather than the view that intelligence is incremental and can be changed and increased by effort and perseverance (see page 11). Students who assimilate an entity view of intelligence primarily see testing as an evaluation of *themselves* rather than as a measure of the skills and competences they have acquired. Highly anxious students have often acquired an entity view of intelligence even before they start school, but classrooms can either reinforce that view or attempt to replace it.

▶ Identifying worries

For students showing anxiety about their inadequacies, it is firstly important for teachers to identify the issues that cause the worry and anxiety. Circle time and other class discussions can address the things students typically worry about and also which individuals within the group have these worries. This helps the teacher to look closely at the environment and attempt to make it less threatening by the way in which tasks are presented and how feedback and evaluation are given.

▶ Supportive and inclusive environments

Many aspects of classroom life are inherently threatening, but how much anxiety is actually experienced depends on how much support and help students feel is available. It is by encouraging supportive and inclusive classrooms that it is acknowledged that we all have strengths and weaknesses. Bullying and peer pressure are the antithesis of the supportive and inclusive classroom, so the constant refrain that we help each other and care for each other is probably the best antidote to anxiety and worry. Buddy systems for support can be invaluable.

▶ **Safe environments**

Teachers themselves need to convey safety – they need to be predictable, so that their behaviour is not hijacked by their own moods of anger, anxiety or depression. The establishment of rules and routines, negotiated jointly and flexibly with the students and non-authoritatively followed through, provides an emotionally secure environment.

Consequences

◼ **Avoid emotional responses**

The way poor behaviour is handled is crucial to the atmosphere of a classroom. Emotionally angry shouting behaviour typically causes more fear and anxiety to other bystanders than it does to the 'perpetrators'. Infringements and violations of rules need to have clearly and previously established consequences. The less emotion the teacher generates, the less is the perceived attack on self-esteem. In emotional states, we are tempted to punish not only the one who has challenged the system but others as well. 'Because of the actions of one, we all have to suffer' is a powerful anxiety-inducing (and anger-inducing) power game that is best avoided.

Teaching personal competences

Some anxieties are reality-based, but the highly anxious student is characterised by faulty thinking that sees threat of attack in objectively quite low-risk situations. Interventions should stress the importance of changing the underlying thinking behind the strongly felt emotions that predispose students to anxious behaviour.

● **Worry bag**

The first step is to identify what things worry the student, maybe by using a 'worry bag'. The student (or students if conducted in a small group setting) writes or dictates his or her problems and worries and puts them into the bag. Some can be taken out and different alternative possible ways of dealing with the concerns discussed, elaborated and tried out through a variety of methods like demonstration, drama and role-play.

● **Problem solving**

Distinguishing the things we do and do not have some control over is very important. Learning to control our own physiology, and therefore the level of emotion experienced, enables us to problem solve much more effectively. It is, therefore, also beneficial to teach problem-solving skills directly. The following framework can be useful in problem solving:

- Ask *'Where am I?'* and *'Where do I want to get to?'*.
- Think of as many ways as possible of reaching that point and evaluate their pros and cons. **Worksheet 8** can be used to help generate alternatives.
- Try out one of the best bets and then evaluate whether and how far 'I' have moved towards where 'I' wanted to get to.

Learning about self-regulation

Knowing and understanding our own emotions is a precondition of being able to manage and handle them, especially those powerful 'negative' emotions of anger and anxiety. These are the emotions that can so easily hijack us into acting inappropriately and in ways that are not in our own (or other people's) longer-term interests. These negative emotions are understood here in terms of a perceived threat and the body's physiological preparation for violent action in terms of heightened arousal. High levels of physiological arousal actually interfere with the blood supply to the brain so that we lose some of the ability to think clearly and to problem solve effectively and become driven by the powerful emotional needs of the moment. The interventions in this section are designed to enable students to manage situations of potentially high arousal – situations where there are perceived serious threats to self-esteem.

The assault or arousal cycle

Studies of what happens to us physiologically in the course of an extreme emotional upset suggest that there is a 'cycle' of events. The stages of this cycle have been described as follows (Breakwell, 1997):

a) The triggering phase

Everyone has a normal or baseline set of non-aggressive behaviours. In this phase, there is a trigger that alerts the person to some threat to their sense of belonging or self-worth and they begin to react physiologically. At this point the person's behaviour indicates a movement away from their baseline. They may become slightly agitated and their facial expression may change. At this stage it may be relatively easy to divert, distract or reassure a younger person.

b) The escalation phase

The person's behaviour deviates more and more from baseline. Physiologically, the individual becomes more and more aroused and all the bodily signs of this become more and more noticeable. Without intervention the person becomes less amenable to diversion and becomes more and more intensely focused on the particular issue.

c) The crisis phase

At this intense point of physiological arousal, the individual will explode into action – either aggressive and assaultive or running away from the situation.

d) The recovery phase

The person's high state of physical and emotional arousal can remain a threat for up to 90 minutes after the incident.

e) The post-crisis depression stage

Mental and physical exhaustion is common and the individual may become tearful, remorseful, guilty, ashamed, distraught or despairing.

● Does not calm down quickly after an upset

Students will feel strong emotions at various times in their school lives. Upsetting emotions involve situations when we become angry, anxious or distressed (and the latter usually involves hurt or loss in some way). We would not expect students to quickly 'get over' bereavement or loss (divorce, separation, loss of a pet or friendship): in fact we might have cause to worry if they did not show much emotion or only for a very short time in such cases. So the interventions here are concerned much more with students who remain angry for long periods of time or show strong emotional reactions of anxiety or distress for objectively rather less serious matters.

Environmental changes

School systems and teachers need to understand the course of the 'arousal cycle' which plots the levels of physiological arousal over the course of the emotional episode (that is release of adrenalin resulting in increased breathing and heart rate, increased muscle tone, sweating and perspiration, dilation of pupils of the eyes, etc.). The more physiologically aroused a person is, the less 'rational' they become: physiologically, for example, the blood supply to the brain is reduced and the brain becomes incoherent and disorganised. Given a perceived threat, levels of arousal climb steeply in the escalation stage until, and unless otherwise checked, they reach the crisis phase when the person becomes aggressively violent or runs away in anxiety.

Following this 'explosion', there is a long and slow plateau or recovery phase where physiological arousal level and felt anger and anxiety only begin to decrease slowly (see page 68). It takes time for the body to begin to return to normal – the length of time seems to increase with age, so is likely to be up to an hour for secondary-aged students. Since physiological arousal levels can remain very high for this long period of time, it is counterproductive and unwise to begin to try to reason or 'problem solve' during the recovery phase of the assault or arousal cycle. It is important to remember that, at high levels of physiological arousal, it is extremely difficult to think straight – and the very good intentions of adults in trying to help work out what happened and why can be very easily misinterpreted, leading to another angry or anxious outburst.

▶ Safe places

What is needed in classrooms and schools is a safe place that is free from questioning and exploration of what happened, and why, by authority figures. Quiet safe zones, where someone is available to simply 'be there' when students have become very angry or distressed, provide an important whole-school intervention. It is very important that arrangements for withdrawing students from classrooms do not place them in 'confrontational' situations immediately after an outburst or episode of very 'difficult' behaviour. Staff asked to work in such situations need to be selected because they are less likely to adopt confrontational attitudes and behaviour themselves.

▶ Calming techniques

Calming measures rather than problem-solving ones are required in the early stages of high arousal. The calming, relaxation and stress reduction techniques described below could be taught to all students within their class setting.

Consequences

Coping with the triggers and the outcomes

Consequences for the behaviour arising from the emotional outbursts should not be discussed or imposed until the student has returned to baseline physiological levels. Until these levels are reached, the response of the staff should be to calm students and to reassure them that they are being listened to and that their intense emotions are acknowledged but not condemned. Although, eventually, it is important that the student faces the reality of his or her behaviour during an explosive incident, when this is being discussed it should be done in a non-emotional matter-of-fact way. The consequences should be presented as the natural or logical outcome of unacceptable behaviour. The problem-solving phase focuses on how the triggers for anger or anxiety can be coped with through less emotionally strong reactions in the future.

Teaching personal competences

Deep breathing

Students, whether angry or anxious, need to acquire strategies for calming themselves and reducing physiological arousal. Calming techniques need to be taught explicitly. Teach slow deep breathing at the rate of approximately six breaths per minute while, at the same time, consciously trying to evoke remembered feelings of affection, tenderness and so on. This technique has demonstrable effects on aspects of heart rate, leading to greater coherence in the functioning of the brain.

Find other calming techniques

To generate alternative strategies for calming themselves, individuals could interview other students or adults to see what strategies they use. Some of these can then be chosen to practise and role-play.

Controlling angry feelings

Distraction techniques (such as exercise or doing another activity), visualising a peaceful enjoyable 'safe place' and meditation techniques can be discussed, demon-strated, practised and monitored. **Worksheet 9** presents a number of strategies that can be used to control angry feelings. These can be discussed and practised in individual counselling sessions or in small group settings.

Prompts to calm down

The teacher may set up a system of prompts to remind students to use the techniques practised to achieve calming. The prompt might be a verbal signal or a card placed unobtrusively or given to the student with an outline (either visually or verbally) of the agreed procedures.

Buddies

The use of a buddy who is also trained in the techniques, as a non-threatening reminder for the need to calm down and how to achieve it, can be helpful.

Therapeutic stories

Therapeutic stories can be written to demonstrate internal cognitive processes that are sometimes difficult to model externally (see page 48 for guidance on using stories).

Gets upset and distressed when fails at something

These interventions primarily address the distress and upset shown by some students when they do not succeed at an activity or in response to comments made by the teacher about the quality of their work. This distress and upset is sometimes shown by displays of crying and expressions of hopelessness, by refusing to take any further part in the activity, or by defacing or throwing away the work they have already produced.

Environmental changes

▶ Praise personal improvements

The first task of the teacher is to be aware of those students who are particularly vulnerable to upset and to notice the first signs of anxiety or distress. It is clear that the way feedback is given needs to be carefully considered for such students and the teacher needs to establish an ethos in the classroom whereby targets are set for effort rather than attainment and praise is given for aspects of student behaviour such as listening, effort and carrying out procedures rather than how well the student has completed the task. An inclusive classroom is one that celebrates success in the improvements over the individual's previous performance rather than one that highlights and ranks students according to attainments.

▶ Clear instructions

It is helpful if teachers try to adopt the viewpoint that they have the responsibility for communicating what the task is about and how to do it. Then, if students do not achieve, it is because the teacher has not been successful in communicating rather than the students' 'fault' for not understanding. This fundamentally non-judgemental response to failure sometimes needs to be expressed quite explicitly by the teacher: *'I'm sorry, I don't think I explained that to you very well'*.

Consequences

■ Don't overprotect

It is important that teachers do not reinforce and reward displays of helplessness. Such displays are a good indication that such students are attempting to defend against their feelings of 'not belonging' by using the strategy of acting in a child-like way and expecting to be 'mothered' so that further demands are not made upon them. It is important that the teacher does not reinforce the strategy by overprotecting the student and 'challenges' the individual. Obviously such challenges require that tasks are just within the student's competence and have been clearly explained, but they need to be accompanied by a firm expectation that the task will be completed.

Teaching personal competences

The distress shown in situations of failure is usually a symptom of low self-esteem and of not really belonging to the community. One of the strategies to preserve the sense of belonging is to signal that the only way we can be worthy of belonging is for somebody to carry us, to do things for us – to become a child who needs to be looked after is the only way we believe we can belong. The student lacks the self-confidence to relate to people if any form of failure is involved.

- **Positive self-talk**

For the student who cries easily in the face of failure, it is important not to belittle or 'attack' the crying as childish. Instead, try to emphasise that it is a strength to be able to express feelings and to be sensitive, and then focus on ways of coping with the difficulty. The teacher should encourage positive self-talk: *'I had difficulty with this, but I can do better next time'*. Provide scenarios where students have negative thoughts about situations of difficulty and help them to generate alternative more positive ways of coping and what they could say to themselves as coping statements: *'I can see he is trying to wind me up, but I am big enough to keep calm and not fall into the trap of losing my temper'*; *'Even if I didn't do very well on that activity, I am still a decent person'*.

The use of cards as self-esteem enhancers with a list of positive self-statements can be useful. In a small group situation, students could be asked to devise such cards for each other. Examples of such self-statements might be: *'I am strong enough to cope with this'* and *'If I plan this out, I am more likely to get the right answer'*.

Is a bad loser

Some students have real difficulty in handling losing at games or competitions. They often then blame other people, get very angry with them and may storm off. If the student loses, it is always construed as somebody else's fault.

Environmental changes

▶ **Classroom culture**

The teacher needs to try to establish a classroom culture which does not promote the notion of students being ranked in terms of value and importance that is linked to success, whether in academic matters or in practical activities or games. The general ethos should be that activities are primarily there to be enjoyed as challenges to developing skills and talents. If value and dignity are linked in students' minds to always winning and being better than someone else, then some individuals, especially those who are unsure of their value and sense of belonging, will react to not winning as an 'attack'. They may then feel that the only way to defend themselves against such an attack is to become aggressive and blame other people, or to preserve their sense of self-esteem by aggressively refusing to take any further part. It is therefore important for the teacher to stress that our worth and value does not depend on winning and to continually focus on the real purpose of competition, which comes from the Latin 'to seek together'. It is primarily an enjoyable challenge to see how well we can do.

▶ **Winning and losing**

Whole-class discussions about good winners and losers and the encouragement of non-competitive as well as competitive games to encourage participation as valuable in its own right are helpful here.

Consequences

When students show anger and aggression at losing, it is important not to respond with aggression or anger and to remember the implications of the arousal cycle – that is, leave the discussions about the unacceptable behaviour until the student has completely calmed down.

■ Teamwork

Be careful not to reward a 'winning at all cost' philosophy, but to focus on reinforcing a co-operative team spirit and working together to achieve success.

Teaching personal competences

● Calming techniques

Particularly in games, the occasion itself produces a release of adrenalin and physiological arousal. That fact alone is likely to mean that students are less rational and more likely to perceive failure as an 'attack'. They may not be in a fit state to problem solve. It is important therefore to teach the student a variety of calming strategies and positive self-talk and to use visualisation to achieve this. **Worksheet 9** suggests some possible strategies to keep control. These use techniques such as distraction (counting slowly to 10, for example) and displacement activities (like drawing a picture). Taking deep breaths is especially powerful when combined with attempts to visualise, in detail, a time when you felt peaceful and content and to try to evoke the feelings you experienced at that time. Rehearsed and practised positive self-statements are also useful, for example: *'I am strong enough to cope with this'*.

● Good sports

The notion of a 'good sport' needs to be directly taught, role-played and practised. Unfortunately there are some very poor role models in professional sport, but there are also an even larger number of very good role models and, on the whole, the most successful sporting heroes have learned how to cope with personal failure and the occasional setbacks: no person, however talented, is 100 per cent successful all the time. Sometimes individuals who are bad losers are particularly prone to taunting by other students who may quite enjoy the spectacle of seeing someone really lose their temper. So particular attention may be necessary to help bad losers cope with such taunting.

● Real-life stories

Positive role models can be used in stories to illustrate how professionals cope with failure. Point out what they might be thinking and saying to themselves when they do not succeed and how they cope with unfairness on the part of other players or decisions going against them.

● Cannot express assertion without losing control

In the face of a threat to self-esteem, there are two reactions that are not helpful to ourselves personally and that do not help in the building up of community. One is a 'fight' response which leads to aggressiveness and the other is a 'flight' response which leads to passive submissive behaviour. In addition, although we have the need and right to protect our own self-worth, we must respect the rights of others to be treated appropriately. Fundamentally, this is about the skills of assertiveness as opposed to aggressive or submissive behaviour.

Environmental changes

▶ **Assertiveness**

The skills of assertiveness, which are crucial to living in a community, need to be modelled, demonstrated and practised in a variety of classroom settings and activities. It is not without significance that *'Assertive Discipline'* was chosen as the title for an approach to classroom management (Canter & Canter, 1997). Whatever the merits and demerits of this particular programme, the title is a good one as the word 'assertive' emphasises the protection and enhancement of both the teachers' rights to have their needs fulfilled at the same time as recognising that students also have rights for their needs to be met.

The teacher therefore needs to model fundamental respect in the way classroom rules are negotiated on the basis of agreed principles and enforced with a primary focus on praise. Any negative consequences being imposed are done without accompanying negative emotions on the part of the teacher, with opportunities and encouragement for reparation rather than an emphasis on 'punishment'.

▶ **Conflict resolution through the curriculum**

Although conflicts are often seen as destructive, there can also be positive aspects. Conflicts can make us more aware of our own and other people's needs and should prompt us to find constructive ways to meet these needs. The taught curriculum should deal explicitly with conflict resolution, focusing on positive aspects of conflict and giving students opportunities to learn the techniques of conflict resolution.

Faced with greater problems of violence, educators in the USA have developed curriculum approaches to teaching conflict-resolution skills, some of which have been designed specifically for secondary-phase students. Some of these materials (for example, *Conflict Busters*) are available from www.incentiveplus.co.uk. It is very important that real-life conflicts in the classroom and in the school grounds become the main opportunities for applying conflict-resolution techniques.

▶ **Conflict-resolution skills**

Students can be asked to generate a list of contexts in which conflicts might occur (for instance, home, classroom, sports field, shops, clubs, etc.) and the people who might be involved (for example, family members, good friends, teachers, students, employers, etc.). They can then write down as many methods as they can think of that people use to try to solve the conflict, identifying those that improve relationships between people and those that often do not solve the problem and leave people feeling angry and devalued.

The *Conflict Resolution Game* (see page 52) is also helpful in this context.

Consequences

I-messages versus you-messages

The teacher needs to be sensitive to the way students handle conflict, annoyances and the irritation of others and can model appropriate responses in the way he or she reacts to anti-social behaviour. The use of I-messages is particularly appropriate in modelling assertive responses to poor behaviour. In essence it focuses on the adult's emotional response to such behaviour: *'I feel ...* [disappointed, let down, frustrated] *when people* (without a personal 'you') *do ...* [a description of the behaviour] *because ...* [a description of how the behaviour is unhelpful to me and others].' This is contrasted with an aggressive you-message that usually starts with 'you' and follows with a personal characteristic rather than a description of the behaviours: *'You are ...* [disobedient, lazy, etc.]'. See page 51 for further information.

Teaching personal competences

Distinguishing assertive, aggressive and passive responses

Students need to be taught to distinguish between assertive, aggressive and passive responses in conflict situations. This can be done using newspaper and magazine pictures, video, role-play, etc. and asking the students to identify the type of response. Positive scripts for handling a variety of typical or personal sources of irritations, annoyances or being on the end of aggressive behaviour can be devised and practised in individual counselling or small group situations. Examples of aggressive and overly passive scripts or role-plays can be used to explore and identify these responses and learn how to replace them with assertive methods.

Assertiveness techniques

Assertion can be taught by the teacher directly modelling and getting the student to practise I-messages (page 51) and other assertiveness techniques (such as the 'broken record', where a request or statement is repeated several times), and how to be assertive in body posture (see Wainwright, 1993).

The 'broken record' method is especially useful if somebody is trying to manipulate or put pressure on you to do something that you really do not want to do. There are three steps to this technique: first, clarify what the other person is trying to get you to do; second, acknowledge the truth of what they are saying or at least their right to that opinion; third, state quite clearly that you do not want to do what is being asked of you.

An example of a teacher modelling the broken record technique might be if a student were to ask, *'Can't we have some fun in this lesson?'*. Having clarified what that student might classify as 'fun', the teacher could say, *'Yes, I can see that would be fun, but I have other plans for this lesson and I want to do that today'*. The students might respond with, *'But we worked so hard yesterday!'* to which the teacher might reply, *'Yes, you did work well last time, but I want to get on and do this today'*. Eventually, people give up. However, because we have shown that we were listening by acknowledging the truth of what the other person has said and because we have been assertive rather than aggressive and have not been 'pushed around', personal relationships have been preserved. The technique clearly has applications to students in handling peer pressure to engage in anti-social or health-damaging behaviour.

● **Language skills**

It is often true that the loss of temper and control in conflict situations is because students have not learned alternative strategies to protect their self-esteem (see example on page 22). Frequently these alternative strategies require the use of language rather than physical engagement. These pragmatic language skills may need to be taught directly to enable the student to use assertive techniques. The interventions related to labelling, recognising and distinguishing between emotions are relevant here (see pages 59 to 63).

● **'Friendly' and 'unfriendly' statements**

In individual or very small group sessions with students who appear to lack sensitivity to the feelings of others, the following activity can be useful. Assertiveness is about being able to express both your positive and negative feelings without being aggressive.

This activity can help students to become more sensitive to the feelings of others by being able to identify what is friendly and unfriendly and by learning to replace unfriendly aggressive statements with friendly assertive ones.

Photocopy **Worksheet 10**, the 'Friendly' and 'Unfriendly' statements. Cut it into separate cards.

- Mix up the cards, blank side up.
- Get the students to pick up a card in turn.
- Encourage the students to decide whether each statement is 'friendly' or 'unfriendly'.
- Encourage discussion about the statements and decisions, role-playing or demonstrating as required.

● Blames others when things go wrong

One of the building blocks of responsible behaviour is the ability to admit that we can make mistakes and thus be able to learn from them. The *'it wasn't me'* response is primarily a defensive one, and the more this becomes an issue between the student and the teacher, the stronger and more adamant denials are likely to become. Sometimes students try to shift the blame on to others, and this obviously has implications for peer relationships.

Environmental changes

▶ **Remove the need for defence**

Denial of responsibility and the blaming of others is a defence against an accusation. No-one likes to be accused, and to accuse someone will almost always put them on the defensive. It is important, therefore, that the teacher does not indulge in accusations. It is useful to have classroom discussions about responsibility and how we sometimes try to get rid of problems of responsibility by shifting the blame on to someone else.

It is also important for the teacher not to interpret denials in the face of the obvious as a challenge to them personally, but to see this denial as a strategy to protect self-esteem. Avoid making an issue out of excuses and avoid confrontations. The more the student is backed into a corner without any other options, the more vehement the denials become. Behaviour change is not about battles to be won or lost or faces being saved or lost.

The primary reason for the teacher to intervene in poor behaviour is not to blame, but to problem solve and to give students strategies and competences to avoid such behaviour in the future.

▶ **Avoid accusatory language**

The language we use can often be subtly accusatory. In this respect it is better for the teacher to avoid using the phrase *'Why* did *you?'*. It is instructive to consider when other people have used this phrase to us – usually we are not asked this question when we have done something good, only when somebody thinks we have done something wrong. And the people asking the question have usually been people such as our parents, teachers or those who have authority over us. These are people whose judgements matter to us and so this can have consequences.

▶ **Non-judgemental approaches**

There is also the fact that, even as adults, we are usually not really able to answer the question about why we have done something, so we can hardly expect students to have such knowledge and understanding. It is a good general principle to only ask questions from which you can expect to get information.

A much more fruitful approach is to try to understand what legitimate needs students are trying to meet by their poor behaviour (see pages 21 to 23 for further information). This is fundamentally a non-judgemental or non-accusatory approach and, because it is non-threatening, the student is much less likely to need to defend his or her self-esteem by denying any responsibility or blaming others.

Consequences

■ **Don't make it a 'big deal'**

When a student misbehaves and breaks rules, consequences are better and more effective if they are small, fast and automatic without argument and without emotion. When 'big deals' are made of things, arguments and denials are more likely and the emotional temperature rises.

■ **Private reprimands**

Wherever and whenever possible, reprimands and aversive consequences should be given as privately as possible to avoid embarrassing the student. In addition to the biological responses to attack, flee or play dead (see page 21), there exists another strategy among the higher mammals. It is sometimes known as the 'flock' response where, in the case of attack, the protection of the 'herd' is sought. Particularly in adolescence, when a teacher reprimands a student in public, there is a tendency for that student to try to get the peer group on his or her side. This is another reason for giving reprimands in private away from the 'herd'.

■ **Focus on good behaviour**

Most denials and shifting the blame are students' strategies to save face, particularly with peers. As a general rule, do not use students' bad behaviour as an exemplar to be held up of how you will handle rule violation. Instead the focus should be on the model behaviour of students as exemplars of how you would like to see them behave. Praising students who tell the truth and admit responsibility for its own sake rather than simply to avoid a more severe punishment is also a useful tactic.

Teaching personal competences

The ability to learn from our mistakes is a foundation stone of the development of being responsible for our actions. Perhaps the most important competence to be acquired is the students' understanding that they are usually trying to meet their legitimate needs, but that there are both appropriate (pro-social) ways of achieving this and inappropriate (anti-social) ways. This is not about the person being good or bad but about choices of different strategies to achieve legitimate ends. Given this view, students are less likely to need to defend themselves and go on to the attack as soon as their behaviour is questioned. The classroom ethos should emphasise that people are not disliked simply because they make mistakes.

● **Using stories**

These skills are cognitive processes, ways of thinking, so they can often be best modelled through stories about how people grow and develop from making mistakes, trying out things which do not work and then looking for other solutions (see page 48 for further information on the use of stories).

● **Learning from mistakes**

Once students understand that they will not be disliked for their mistakes, activities such as circle time or writing activities can be used for the students to consider the following statement: *'A time when I made a mistake was ... and I learned ... from it'*.

● **A 'no blame' approach**

A focus on a 'no blame' approach to problems should characterise classrooms when there are behaviour problems – what was the person trying to do, what were the consequences of what they did do, what were the feelings of the individual on the receiving end, and what would then be useful thoughts and feelings for the person who realises they have behaved badly?

Increasing motivation

Motivation is very closely linked to emotion. The skills and competences in this section deal with the way emotions are used to foster the achievement of personal, academic and pro-social goals. It certainly involves the notion of resilience where a person is able to bounce back and get themselves back on track after difficult emotional experiences, including disappointment, frustration, failure, dashed expectations and loss. It also involves an emotional 'toughness' or persistence in the face of difficulty, distractions and the needs of the moment. If a difficult task can be perceived as a challenge rather than a threat, we are more able to problem solve, work out the pros and cons of our actions and have a realistic appraisal of likely outcomes. The interventions in this section relate to reducing negative emotions, which increases the likelihood that we will persist with tasks and remain motivated.

There are essentially three stages of motivation – getting started, staying with the task, and finishing off the task well. Getting started is often the problem of procrastination, where anything else is more attractive than the task in hand. Staying with the task is about persisting in the face of distractions and having a plan that is being followed despite the temptation to give up. Sometimes students near the end of the task, but then 'rubbish' what they have done and give up at the last minute.

Procrastinates or leaves things to the last minute

Sometimes people work more efficiently when under pressure so, in rare cases, leaving things to the last minute may result in achievement of the task. On the whole, however, procrastination generally increases stress, lessens efficiency and is a major contribution to lowering educational outcomes. Procrastination is not simply a problem in study skills but has much wider implications for life generally – it can lead to all kinds of negative emotions, including guilt, low self-esteem and depression.

Environmental changes

Students do not achieve what we know them to be capable of when they are disorganised and when they cannot recognise the priorities and carry these tasks out. The first step in these cases is to try to understand why a student is disorganised as this may help to determine what kind of interventions might be useful.

Teachers need to be aware of the potential seriousness of the habit of procrastination for their students and therefore to address the issue directly in the way tasks are presented and work is monitored. The older the student the more scope there is for choice as to when and how things are done, and therefore for procrastination, but it is important for this to be seen as a potential obstacle to success from an early age.

► **Six reasons for procrastination**

Six different motives or reasons for procrastination have been identified and so the type of intervention may well depend upon the particular reason. So it is important for teachers to try to understand why particular students have a problem in this area.

1. A basic reason for procrastination is a lack of skills for carrying out a task. Lack of skills makes a task very difficult and we tend to avoid things that we see as very difficult. It is emotionally sometimes hard to do things that expose a lack of skill. For example, a poor reader will tend to avoid tasks that involve reading. Improving requisite skills and confidence in them for achieving tasks is likely to reduce the need to procrastinate.

2. We tend to avoid tasks that we find boring and which do not interest us. The fact is that in school, as in any other work, there are aspects that we find boring and monotonous. The teacher's task is to encourage interest and relevance but, in the final analysis, there are some tasks we simply have to do. Because a task is not intrinsically interesting, it may require extrinsic 'carrots' and the application of 'Grandma's Law' – namely, you have to eat the vegetables you do not like before you get the fruit which you do like.

3. Some people procrastinate because they have the mistaken belief that they must feel motivated before starting a task. Often it is only when we start a task that we then become motivated to carry it through. Once we have started something, we are then motivated to finish it off because if we do not finish it we have wasted considerable time and effort. 'Get started' is the technique teachers need to encourage when a task has been given.

4. Many students procrastinate, not because of an objective lack of skill, but because of poor self-esteem. It is emotionally less secure and seen as an attack on our self-esteem to have tried hard to do something and to have failed, but it is much easier and safer not to have tried because then there is no failure. By procrastinating, the perfectionist defends him or herself against the possibility of failure being due to lack of cleverness or competence because the failure can interpreted as being due to something outside the control of the person like lack of time: *'I would have done better if I had more time, but I didn't give myself enough time'*.

5. Just occasionally, it is not fear of failure that leads to putting things off to the last minute, but the fear of success. To succeed may actually increase pressure on us to do even better next time. This is especially true in relation to parental pressure – emotionally it may be safer not to do so well, and one of the subtle ways of not doing well is to procrastinate. Teachers may fall into the same trap: *'Well done for completing that work so quickly and well. Here's another dose!'*.

6. Finally, a tendency to procrastinate can be an emotional tactic to avoid being 'pushed around'. It may be a tactic to cope in a power struggle, a way of asserting one's own sense of control and independence. Again, this may be in relation to parents rather than teachers, but can certainly involve teachers who are rather 'authoritarian' in their attitudes. Leaving things to the last minute is sometimes therefore a subtle, and sometimes not so subtle, message that *'You do indeed have more power than I have, but I'll use the little power that I do have!'*.

► **Goal setting**

The first question to ask is whether the students actually know what needs to be done: if they do not, no other tactics to help them carry out necessary tasks will be of much use. Students need to be taught how to establish what the priorities are – this relates to goal planning and setting which is an essential part of study skills. The curriculum needs to address these issues directly rather than assuming that they will simply be picked up along the way. Teachers can model and demonstrate their own goal-setting techniques by clearly establishing and communicating the structure, nature and purpose of all that they do themselves and ask students to do.

Many students do not set goals and establish priorities because they have not been introduced to the idea of goal setting as being a factor in their success. Goal setting is an essential part of problem solving: *'Where am I now?'* and *'Where do I want to get to?'*. Problem-solving methods usually start with big goals, which are translated into long-term goals and then broken down into short-term goals – that is, quite specific things that need to be done.

Once students realise that goal setting is important, they should then be taught to do it. Teaching goal setting involves demonstrating it, providing plenty of opportunities for practising the skills in everyday life and giving feedback on how well goal setting has been carried out in practice. The very simple 'plan, do, review' procedure (see 'Rewards' below and see page 14) needs to be at the heart of every activity students do in school and should be repeated often so that it becomes internalised and automatic. This applies right across the spectrum of the abilities as it is just as essential, if not more so, for students having difficulties (either cognitive or emotional).

Consequences

■ **Rewards**

As always, it is important to focus acknowledgement and praise precisely towards those behaviours you wish to see more of. In this case, therefore, the focus is not on attainment of the task but on the effort put into applying and using the framework of goal setting: namely, analysing the task into what needs to be done (plan), and faithfully carrying out and checking what actually is done (do) against the plan (review). It is here that the motivational aspect of behaviour is important and may explain why students are disorganised – they know *what* to do, *how* to do it and have been given *practice* and *feedback* in doing it, but the task is not done because it is not *worth their while*. Emotions and low-frustration tolerance can hijack us from carrying out our plans. Rewards are important in shifting the balance of long-term gains against short-term costs.

Teaching personal competences

● **Avoiding procrastination**

This activity is designed to help students who tend to put a task off, particularly if it does not capture their interest or is perceived to be difficult; because it is perceived to be difficult, negative emotions produced by this perception prevent students from doing necessary tasks.

Discuss with an individual the activities he or she finds difficult to tackle. With the student develop a story that includes this information (see page 48 for further information on the use of stories).

Discuss with the student:

- what helped the person in the story to do things, for instance, knowing what to do;
- what stops the person from doing things, for instance, being unsure what to do.

Write the ideas on to cards and use boxes labelled 'What helps us ...' and 'What stops us ...' to reinforce the concept.

● Mind mapping

Prioritising and planning are important in problem solving. If leaving things to the last minute is an outcome of not really understanding the task and the steps needed to complete it, then the strategies given above for goal setting should be used first.

Planning an activity can involve the use of a 'mind map' as a tool to improve a student's ability to prioritise and plan a project. Mind maps were developed by Buzan (1993) as a whole-brain approach to improving learning, taking notes and planning activities. They are sometimes known as 'concept maps', 'spider-writing' or 'brain-webs'. Mind maps are particularly useful for helping to organise a project and they do not require extensive literacy skills since they use imagery and symbols as well as words.

The central theme is usually placed in a circle in the centre of the page. Then keywords are used to represent ideas and these are connected to the central theme with lines. Colour, images and symbols can be used to highlight priorities, etc. Computer programs for mind mapping are also available (for example, *Inspiration*, see www.inspiration.com/index.cfm).

● Overcoming obstacles

Worksheet 11 may be photocopied and used if desired. Working in a small group or individually, the students are asked to identify a difficult goal that they would like to achieve. Write this in the 'goal' box at the top of the 'stairs' on the worksheet. Then ask the students to identify four or five short-term goals that would have to be achieved in order to reach the goal at the top of the stairs. At each step, the students should also think of some obstacles that might make it difficult to reach the next step. Get them to brainstorm possible solutions to each obstacle, filling in the worksheet as they proceed.

● Is unable to shut out distractions and focus on a task

There are two main types of distractibility:

- a rather passive 'daydreaming' where the student seems to focus on internal thought processes rather than the task in hand;
- a more active type when the student responds to each and every stimulus, except that of the task being set – this tends to be linked to impulsivity and hyperactivity.

Both types tend not to do well in academic learning, with the latter also tending to disrupt the learning of others as well as their own. However, the aim of any intervention for both groups is the same – to increase engaged time on a task – as this has been shown to be a vital variable in raising learning outcomes.

Environmental changes

▶ **Passive distractibility**

For the passive 'daydreamer', it is especially important to uncover the need that the student is attempting to meet by not focusing on the task. Frequently such students are attempting to defend a fragile sense of self-worth: they have often experienced 'failure' and have given up trying, and so retreat into a learned helplessness. This is sometimes rooted in a view of themselves as stupid and incompetent and seeing achievement as something 'fixed' and given. The teacher needs to model the view that effort is the most important factor in classrooms rather than intelligence or cleverness. Praise and recognition should therefore be consciously directed to effort and improvement over previous performance as a result of effort. The passively distractible student needs to be challenged with a careful match between where the student is and the small next step, with excuses not accepted. The approach should certainly not reinforce the helplessness with overprotectiveness.

▶ **Active distractibility**

For the active distractible student, it is often useful to limit visual and auditory distractions as much as possible. The student needs to be explicitly involved in this process as its aim is to be helpful rather than punitive (but it may well appear to be punitive if there is no student involvement). It is useful if the student's physical location, that is the classroom, can be the least distracting possible and the size of the immediate group is smaller rather than larger, with only immediately needed materials placed on the desk or table. Clear instructions from the teacher are essential and these should be broken down into small discrete steps, avoiding 'chain' commands (namely those that contain one instruction followed by another and yet another).

Students who are easily distracted can be construed as having very low-frustration tolerance (see page 85) or an inability to tolerate delay.

▶ **Model organisational skills**

Teachers need to model systematic organisation through their own tasks, breaking tasks down and working through 'checklists'. Lessons need to have clearly visible structures of activities and transitions. It is useful if teachers can actually make explicit their thought processes and how they are working through the task of organisation.

Consequences

■ **Clear targets**

For the active distractible student, small precise targets need to be clearly specified, with prompts and cues to enable the student to achieve these. These prompts and cues, often very visual, are there to help the student work through a given task. Rules need to be clear especially for these students, with positive rewards directed primarily to effort in staying on a task rather than for attainment.

Contracts

A behavioural contract, particularly with the involvement of home, is often useful. There is some research evidence to suggest that over-active and very impulsive individuals may need the additional structure of 'penalties', that is starting off with a bank or credit of rewards which can be lost by inappropriate behaviour. See page 52 for further information on contracts.

Concrete rewards

Both active and passive distractibility need to be rewarded for effort, and this should reflect general classroom and school policy. An inclusive school is one that recognises the diversity of individual differences and acknowledges effort rather than just attainment. By setting individual targets and rewarding efforts in achieving these, all students will feel valued equally. The more visual and concrete rewards, such as points and graphs, are especially useful.

Teaching personal competences

Listening skills are important when focusing on tasks. (For some tasks focusing on listening skills, see pages 87 and 91.) In addition, there is a need to filter out visual distractions when focusing on an activity.

Writing and avoiding distractions

This activity can be used with individuals or small groups.

To help improve students' ability to filter out visual distractions when completing a written task, the students are given a puzzle to complete that requires them to focus on visual information and to ignore visual distractions. For example, the students are required to circle the numbers 3 and 2 when they appear together and in that order, as below. **Worksheet 12** may be photocopied and used if desired.

3 2 1 4 9 6 3 2 3 4 2 1 3 2 5 ...

This activity can be extended into finding a small item in a large picture, to 'odd one out' activities and wordsearches. Materials can be adapted in a variety of ways to gradually increase the complexity of the task and to make it age-appropriate. The *Somerset Thinking Skills Course* (Blagg, *et al.*, 1988) contains some useful materials and activities. These were developed to teach specific concepts and skills involved in problem solving and learning to learn. The first of seven modules, entitled *Foundations for Problem Solving*, includes activities designed to reduce impulsivity and to enhance scanning and focusing in order to solve a problem.

Cannot complete a task

Some students start off a task or activity, sometimes with enthusiasm and sometimes impulsively, but rarely then see the task through to the end. Aspects of persistence, putting up with routine work or sometimes 'boring' detail are involved here.

Environmental changes

The environmental needs will differ to some extent depending on the nature of the student's motives for not completing the task. Therefore, the first task of the teacher is to understand some of the reasons why students may start activities or tasks and then give them up. For example:

- The student is very impulsive, does not listen or focus on what the task really involves and so, having started, quickly finds that he or she does not know what to do and so gives up.
- The student has listened and understood the task but has a low-frustration tolerance and may well do the initial or interesting bits of the task, but then the needs of the moment are more attractive than the longer time commitment to finish it off.
- The student is apathetic and unmotivated, so begins the task but is not at all concerned about how far he or she gets with it or about the quality of the material produced.

▶ Checklists

For the very impulsive student who rushes into things without listening, it is important to ensure that his or her attention is directly sought and held, with an explicit instruction to not begin work until a specific signal has been given. This instruction should become routine for the teacher. In addition, the task needs to be spelled out very clearly. It is often useful if the student writes down keywords or symbols about the process of the task or activity and uses this as a checklist to work through.

▶ Tailor-made tasks

For the more generally apathetic, bored and unmotivated student, it is crucially important that tasks are made as personally relevant as possible, using themes and interests that are tailor-made to the individual. It is important for the teacher to try to understand what legitimate needs the student is protecting by being bored and apathetic.

To be able to follow a task through to completion will initially involve short tasks with clear beginnings and endings. Students need to know what they are doing, where to begin and how they will know when they have finished.

Consequences

Rewards

Rewards should be given in the first instance to students *attempting to follow* the procedures and techniques that have been established to help them persist with a task that they would normally give up on. For the impulsive student, rewards and praise should be directed to success in waiting for instructions, developing an outline of what needs to be done, etc. For the student with low-frustration tolerance, praise and recognition should be given to following through the procedures as well as for the actual completion of the task.

Teaching personal competences

Changing self-statements

Low-frustration tolerance may be the result of 'dysfunctional thinking', where children and young people are saying to themselves things like: *'I can't do this, I'm totally hopeless'*, *'This is really boring, I must do something more interesting'*, *'I can't stand this any longer'*. If they are thinking in this way, it is not surprising that they feel as if they must just give up. Dysfunctional self-statements need to be replaced with more appropriate ones like: *'This is really difficult, but not impossible'*, *'Do a little bit more, Rome wasn't built in a day'*. Working with an individual student, it is necessary to generate a number of inappropriate self-statements and then replace them, with practice, with more appropriate and helpful ones. The theory behind this suggests it is our thinking that profoundly influences how we feel, and it is our feelings that make us give up. If you can change the self-statements (thinking), this may change the feelings and subsequently the behaviour.

Real-life histories of famous people who have achieved great things despite physical difficulties, opposition from powerful people or feeling discouraged, could be researched and written up. Similarly, personalised therapeutic stories to illustrate the themes could be composed (see page 48 for further information on the use of stories). Questions to ask might be: *'What obstacles needed to be overcome, how were these overcome, and what were the self-statements and thinking which kept "the hero or heroine" going through the difficult or rough times?'*.

Proformas

For the student with low-frustration tolerance and with difficulties about particular aspects of the task, a specific framework or proforma may be helpful to work through the task. An example of this type of framework is given in **Worksheet 13**.

Enhancing empathy

The ability to see the world from another's point of view is a fundamental requirement for effective communication. In fact, communication is only achieved when there is a sharing and acknowledgement of each other's viewpoints. It begins with the ability to listen – for without listening we can never learn what somebody else is thinking and feeling. Listening to other people is the prerequisite for showing care and concern, and thus is the first necessary step to building community.

Talks too much and does not listen

It is important to recognise that there is a real difference between students who are so concerned about their own needs that they talk too much and do not listen to other people and naturally very talkative students who *do* listen to what others have to say. We find that the former tend not to be liked by other students: they do not ask questions, for example, which seems to be a very important skill for joining a group; they appear arrogant and to be a 'know all' to their peers who then tend to reject them. The students who have a lot to say but who do communicate listening are frequently well-liked and popular as they often have lots of ideas.

Environmental changes

▶ **Discover the student's legitimate need**

The first task of the teacher is to consider the possible reasons for a student's need to talk too much: what legitimate need is he or she trying to protect? Young people have a legitimate need to be noticed, but for some students this means that they have to dominate, which is not the same thing. It may be that the legitimate need for 'control' and 'choice' is achieved by strategies that involve excessively controlling the agenda by continually talking – this may be perceived as being more predictable and therefore safer.

▶ **Modelling listening**

The teacher is a powerful model of the balance between the need to communicate our needs and wishes and requests and our duty to listen to other people. The teacher who does not listen or 'let students get a word in edgeways', who nags on and on when they misbehave and who, having asked a question, does not leave students real space to answer it, reminds us that the power and authority of teachers makes them particularly vulnerable to modelling the very behaviour that we do not wish to see students adopting.

▶ **Speaking and listening rules**

Much effective classroom organisation consists of providing a framework in which students can speak and listen at appropriate times. This ability is particularly important in a large group setting such as the classroom. There need to be clearly negotiated and articulated 'rules' for getting the balance right between speaking and listening. It is useful for teachers to develop clear signals for when they expect the class to pay attention to what they have to say. Moving to a particular place in the classroom space for formal whole-class instructions and adopting a particular body posture are effective ways that teachers can use to communicate listening expectations. Explicit rules for how and when students can communicate with the teacher and with each other in whole-class situations are also necessary.

In certain group settings such as circle time, the fundamental balance between speaking and listening may be fostered by using particular procedures – for instance, it is a person's turn to speak when they are holding a particular object.

Consequences

Reinforcing speaking and listening behaviour

The way that teachers notice and acknowledge appropriate speaking and listening behaviour is more important than the way they respond to rule-breaking behaviour in this instance. This means specifically praising appropriate behaviour and describing clearly how that behaviour has been useful. Just as I-messages are useful when dealing with inappropriate behaviour, they are also ideal when noticing and acknowledging appropriate behaviour: *'I like it when students put up their hands when they want to say something because it makes it easier for me to hear what they are saying or to know which way to look when somebody wants to speak'*. See page 51 for more information about I-messages.

Rule-breaking behaviours in the area of speaking and listening within a classroom are among those lower level 'drip-drip' behaviours that cause teachers irritation and stress. However, they are precisely those behaviours where it is generally more effective to ignore the rule-breaking while at the same time responding to instances of appropriate behaviour so that they are noticed and acknowledged before reprimanding any inappropriate behaviour.

Teaching personal competences

Emotion stories

In a small group setting, with younger students, use a story such as 'A day in the life of Zoë' opposite. Explain that the students must first listen carefully to a story because they will be asked questions about it afterwards. The story is then read to the group. In turn, each student picks a prepared card which asks who showed a particular emotion. The cards focus on emotions rather than on factual details, for example: *'Who was …* [calm]*?'*. The following emotions can be included: happy, sad, lonely, scared, frustrated, proud, relaxed, loving, jealous, aggressive, calm, angry, excited, guilty, nervous. The precise emotions and vocabulary involved will vary according to the emotional literacy level of the group. The student who has chosen a card points at another member of the group (who must make eye contact to show that he or she is listening) and asks the other person the question on the card. The answer given will indicate whether or not he or she has been listening. The process is repeated in turn until all the question cards have been used.

A day in the life of Zoë

- Zoë gets up. She is feeling excited because it is the weekend and she is meeting her friends.
- She goes to the cupboard to get out the cereal for breakfast and she is angry because her brother has eaten the last of her favourite cereal.
- The cat brushes past her leg and she feels calm again because the cat was very loving towards her.
- As Zoë goes outside, she is very happy because her mother has given her some extra money to spend with her friends.
- She meets up with Jack first. He is looking fed up. He explains it is because his mother has refused to give him any money to spend today because he hasn't tidied his room.
- Zoë decides to buy him a drink. This brings a smile to Jack's face. Zoë feels proud because she has been kind.
- They walk together and come across a boy all on his own. He has argued with his friends and now is feeling lonely.
- He has fallen out with his friends because he refused to allow another boy to play football with them. He is now feeling guilty about this.
- Now he is on his own and his friends have gone off to play with the boy he did not include. He is feeling jealous of him now and wished he had done things differently.

Is insensitive to the feelings of others

Empathy is the product of the skills of listening, and is concerned more with the feelings that are being communicated rather than with the descriptive facts. It is quite possible for a student to be able to repeat the facts that have been expressed, while at the same time being quite insensitive to the feelings that the other person is experiencing. If there is an absence of communication at the feelings level, it is highly probable that the student will misread interpersonal situations which may lead to isolation and rejection by peers or to squabbles and conflicts.

There can be a variety of possible reasons why students are insensitive to the feelings of others, but it is frequently the case that such individuals are 'frightened' of expressing any emotion or see the expression of emotions as weak, silly or childish. If they do not allow themselves to express either positive or negative emotions, or both, it is highly likely that they will not be able to read other people's emotions either. The inability to read such emotions will frequently mean that they will misinterpret the social task they have to solve. Most of our interpersonal interactions can be construed as problem solving. Dodge (1999) has identified a number of recurring types of situations that are problematic for students in school. Emotionally literate students have the ability to correctly read the situation, come up with a variety of possible solutions, choose one of these and learn from this experience. If a student is unable to read and acknowledge the emotions others are experiencing, he or she will have great difficulty in coping with the emotional demands of life in school.

Environmental changes

▶ **Expressing emotions in the classroom**

It is important in the daily life of classrooms to express concern for emotions – how I feel, how others feel and the effects of this on how I and others behave. General curriculum activities together with interventions such as circle time, no blame approaches to bullying, circle of friends and so on are all fundamentally trying to address the problem of how we can develop skills and understandings of how other people feel and what it is like to feel the way that others feel. The ideas behind the interventions mentioned here, if not the precise procedures themselves, need to permeate classroom life. It will help to achieve this if teachers focus on their own sensitivity to students' emotions in relation to the teachers and their work and if they model this appropriately to the class. When there are issues of bullying, interpersonal conflict and students becoming obviously emotional, there are opportunities for the teacher to examine with the class how people feel. In addition, drama, stories, poetry and other literature, art and music may also be vehicles to explore how it is to feel and thereby increase sensitivity to others' feelings.

Consequences

■ **Reinforcing appropriate behaviour**

Behaviour that is indicative of an understanding and sensitivity to people's feelings needs to be noticed, acknowledged and rewarded. I-messages, either in public or preferably in private, can be an appropriate format for rewarding appropriate behaviour, where a student has shown sensitivity to the feelings of others. See page 51 for further information about I-messages.

■ **Dealing with bullying**

Bullying is best approached by attempting to increase the sensitivity of bullies to the effects of their behaviour on how others feel rather than by punishment, as they have frequently had a surfeit of that in their own lives. It is often the case that a non-judgemental approach to the bully, that conveys the assumption that the bully and the bystanders have not fully appreciated how others feel when they treat them in a certain way, is more effective than assuming an inherent 'nastiness' in the bully. The distinction between the *behaviour* (which is unacceptable, hurtful to others and destructive of community) and the *person* is of paramount importance here.

To enable an increased measure of sensitivity to the effects of bullying actions, those who have been bullied can be encouraged to express in a variety of possible media how they are feeling and the effects of the behaviour of others towards them. Feelings cannot be disputed: facts about who did what and who started it frequently can be and are disputed – it can be counterproductive, and often impossible, to separate out cause and effect.

Teaching personal competences

● **Acts of kindness**

It can be helpful to demonstrate to the students how other people react when treated with empathy and sensitivity. **Worksheet 14**, the 'Acts of kindness log', can be photocopied and used by the students.

● **'Friendly' and 'Unfriendly' statements**

The activity presented on page 76 and in **Worksheet 10** can also be used here to support students in becoming more sensitive to the feelings of others.

● **Listening for feelings**

In a very small group, help students to identify an occasion (which they are prepared to share) when the individual felt a strong 'negative' emotion (such as anger, anxiety, etc.). Then ask each of them to tape record or video themselves telling an imaginary friend about the incident, what happened and how they felt.

Having listened to or watched the account, each member of the group writes or records a message back to the person, trying to convey that they understand how it must have felt. Students can be taught some rudimentary active listening skills (such as reflecting back, paraphrasing and summarising) and then practise these.

Improving social skills

Emotional literacy depends upon the ability to recognise and understand our own emotions and the emotions of others. This is the ability to read the situation, to make sense of what is going on or to determine the interpersonal and emotional task that needs to be solved. The next step is to be able to generate a number of solutions, and the final step is to carry out that 'best bet' for solving the task which preserves both our own and the other person's self-esteem.

The emotionally literate student is able to carry out each of these steps and so to act in a pro-social way and, thereby, to build community. It is quite possible for a student to have read a situation correctly, to have determined what is an appropriate behaviour and still not have the skills and competences to actually carry it out. The dimension of 'social skills' refers to the student's abilities to carry out those behaviours that are the product of previously reading the situation and of generating a number of possible alternatives.

● Does not laugh and smile when appropriate

Smiling and laughter are 'infectious' and so are misery and gloom! Students relate well to each other and become involved in the group to the extent that they communicate a range of appropriate emotions. This skill is not concerned with a false cheerfulness or the neurotic tendency to avoid pain and sadness and cover it up with a false bonhomie. It may, however, have some resonance with the findings that optimists relate better to other people and are more liked.

Environmental changes

▶ **A positive atmosphere**

Research into classroom climates suggests that students prefer classrooms in which there is more co-operation and friendship, where the work is perceived as challenging but not too difficult, and where there is pace and variety (for example, see Fraser, *et al.*, 1982). All these elements lead to a 'lighter' and more positive atmosphere in the classroom.

▶ **Emotionally literate teachers**

Teachers tend to be liked when they are perceived to have a sense of humour and can laugh with the students, but certainly not at them. Emotionally literate teachers can laugh at themselves, smile a great deal and know when it is appropriate to be serious and when it is appropriate to laugh and smile. If teachers like young people, and this again appears to be a crucially important perception for students to have of their teachers, they inevitably quite comfortably display a range of emotions, including those of laughter and humour. It is difficult if teachers are themselves under considerable stress to demonstrate such emotions spontaneously – perhaps the key environmental change required here is the way the school itself values and supports its teaching and non-teaching staff. Classrooms often reflect staffrooms!

Consequences

■ **Give clear expectations of behaviour**

Students who are not liked by their peers, for whatever reason, are especially vulnerable to being laughed at and made fun of by their fellow students. There is a big difference between a classroom in which there is mutual fun and enjoyment and one where 'fun' is taken at other people's expense. Being laughed at is a profoundly hurtful and demeaning experience for children and young people. Teachers need to explore these issues with their students and have clear expectations that such behaviour will be treated seriously.

However, it is probably more useful to respond to students laughing at other students, particularly in relation to academic or social gaffes, privately rather than publicly. Quiet words of reassurance to the 'victim' are likely to be appreciated more than making an issue of it publicly, which often adds to the embarrassment and hurt. Similarly, addressing these issues privately afterwards with the students responsible for the hurt and embarrassment is generally more helpful, provided of course the teacher conveys disapproval by short factual re-statement of the rules of acceptable behaviour in this matter at the time of the incident. The paramount duty of the class teacher is always to ensure the emotional, as well as the physical, safety of the students.

■ **Shaping behaviour**

For students who appear to be excessively 'serious', the usual strategies of shaping apply – that is, noticing and praising more appropriate ways of acting, when the student does smile or laugh appropriately.

Teaching personal competences

A student who is rarely seen to laugh or smile should sound some alarm bells as a possible indication of a seriously unhappy or depressed individual. Depression can range from mild, through moderate to severe and reflects the degree to which the students have come to see themselves, the world around them, or the future as helpless and hopeless. It is a concern that sometimes even very seriously depressed individuals are not noticed for what they are and it is important that teachers alert parents of their concerns and the possible need for specialist mental health input when a student's low mood is significantly interfering with his or her taking part in the activities of normal school life.

● **Finding the positives**

Students with low mood need to be encouraged to see themselves and their world differently and teachers can help to shift the focus away from helplessness and hopelessness by focusing on the positive in all their interactions with the student. Low mood is primarily due to a very selective attention to the negative aspects of themselves – positives are simply not noticed or are ignored. The teacher can help the individual to draw up lists of his or her positive attributes, achievements and pleasant experiences and can then encourage the student to rehearse these, even on a daily basis. This can help students to become more aware of the positives in their lives.

Setting achievable goals

It is also useful to help students set themselves tailor-made, realistic and attainable work and social goals. They should then be encouraged to evaluate their own work by *first* finding four positives about it. Following that they can identify 'improvement suggestions' (not failures or mistakes).

Group work on when to laugh

For the more general issue of teaching individuals when it is appropriate to laugh and smile, some one-to-one or small group work around the following topics is useful:

- What makes you laugh or smile?
- How do you know someone finds something funny?
- Does everyone find the same things funny? Why not?
- Are there times when you smile or laugh when things aren't really funny? Why might this be?
- Are there times when laughing or smiling might upset people? How do you know this has upset them?

The following activity can be used during the above discussions; **Worksheet 15** can be used for this activity if desired. The worksheet gives three scenarios in which a person might smile or laugh and the student must complete the worksheet with concrete personal examples of each scenario.

Does not ask for help when appropriate

Students may be reluctant to ask for help when they need it for a variety of reasons. The first task of the teacher is to attempt to uncover the motives of the student – that is, why he or she does not ask for help or which legitimate need the student is trying to protect or fulfil by not asking for help. This will provide the best guide to the most appropriate intervention.

One of the motives for not asking for help may be shyness and embarrassment based on the belief that to be seen asking for assistance is to expose oneself as incompetent or stupid. Asking for help is often a public act in relation to the peer group, and the need to protect one's relationships in the group may be dominant. Students who are very withdrawn and shy hate to be noticed in public and asking for help often involves speaking up in public settings. However, even when protected from peers, asking for help may be seen as an admission of incompetence to the teacher.

Another common motive for not requesting help can be summed up in words such as *'apathetic, bored, indifferent, I don't care anyway'*. The unwillingness to ask for help is then an expression of a wider malaise or disaffection from school.

Environmental changes

For the unmotivated, disaffected student, all the strategies for helping such individuals are applicable here. Many of these students will not have experienced any success academically and so will 'switch off' as a way of preserving their own self-worth: if you do not try, you cannot be accused of failing.

More difficult are those students whose interest is profoundly affected by a peer culture (especially in boys), in which it is not 'cool' to show any interest in schoolwork. These are important whole-school issues, including for example the availability of male role models.

▶ **Responding to requests for help**

The way the teacher responds to requests for help may have a strong influence on whether students ask for help or not: for example, teachers may sometimes respond to requests in a way that conveys the impression that there is some fault in the student that has prompted the need to ask for help. Because of the inherent power imbalance in teacher-student relationships, it is important that teachers act in ways that explicitly convey the opposite impression. It is helpful for teachers to adopt the attitude that, when a student has misunderstood the nature of the task, this is due to the teacher's failure to communicate effectively rather than the student's failure to understand: '*I don't think I've really explained that very well ...*' rather than '*If you had listened carefully, you would know what to do*'.

A classroom climate in which the teacher genuinely attempts to see positive motives for students' questions and which does not 'parade' the teacher's superior knowledge is likely to produce appropriate questioning by students, for example praising those who ask questions and trying to express back to them positive aspects of the question.

▶ **Privacy in asking for help**

For shy and easily embarrassed students, the teacher who moves around the classroom, and so enables personal rather than obviously public communication, is more likely to foster the skills of asking questions in such students.

▶ **Classroom management techniques**

To reduce the likelihood of misunderstanding, the teacher needs to ensure that:

- the instructions given are clear;
- there is a clear signal that an instruction is to be followed, making eye contact with all students before an instruction is given;
- the instruction has been understood by asking students to repeat back what they have to do;
- students do not start an activity until a precise indication to do so has been given.

Consequences

Responding to questioning behaviour

Teachers need to be very careful not to punish questioning behaviour and to remember that ignoring behaviour is a way of extinguishing it. Students should be praised for asking questions when it is appropriate to do so with the teacher seeking out the positives in any question and communicating these positives back to the student. There should be space and permission for asking questions. A student who is put down or demeaned for asking a question is unlikely to ask another, except if a function of the questioning is to fulfil his or her legitimate need for attention. In this case, alternative strategies to fulfil that need should be encouraged.

Teaching personal competences

Asking for help

Some of the following discussion points can be explored with individuals, with small groups or with whole classes in settings such as circle time:

- When might you need to ask for help?
- Who could you ask for help?
- How can you ask for help?
- When is it difficult to ask for help?
- What can you do if you are not able to get help straight away?

Sort and match cards

Use a range of situation cards and range of response cards, such as those shown in **Worksheet 16**. This worksheet can be photocopied on to card and cut up. The student is presented with a situation card and chooses an appropriate response from the set offered. The adult and student discuss why the response was chosen. The response cards are returned to the set after each turn so that they can be picked again.

Feelings bingo

Feelings bingo is best played in small groups. Photocopy **Worksheet 17** and give each student a bingo board and some small squares of paper with which to cover up the emotion words shown on their board. The adult has a set of cards to match the emotions on the boards, selected and cut up from **Worksheet 18**, and chooses one of the feelings at random. The students can cover up the word on their board only when they have been able to say something about the emotion depicted – for example, when he or she felt like this, when people normally feel this emotion, how you might be able to cope with it. 'Bingo' is called when a student completes his or her board.

Please note that examples of boards are given on **Worksheet 17** for you to photocopy and use. However, you may wish to make your own boards from the set of words provided in **Worksheet 18** to suit the vocabulary of your particular students. Other emotion words can be selected, as desired, from **Worksheet 1**. Extra boards for larger groups can be made in the same way.

Is unable to effectively discriminate a range of feelings

This has something in common with the ability to label and describe various emotions, and several of the interventions described on pages 61 to 63 are appropriate here.

Environmental changes

The classroom needs to become an environment in which feelings are seen to matter and can be discussed.

▶ **Weekly emotions**

Focus on particular emotions in the curriculum on a week-by-week basis, using various aspects of the taught curriculum to help define, discriminate and recognise different emotions. For example, an emotion (like anger, jealousy or excitement) could become the subject of an assembly, stories illustrating aspects of the emotion could be used in literacy activities, and an exemplar of the emotion could be discussed in history.

▶ **Model**

Teachers can model their own emotional states or reactions and can also give feedback to students as to how they perceive them to be feeling.

▶ **I-messages**

The use of I-messages is an appropriate way of communicating the effect on us of other people's behaviour. See page 51 for more information.

▶ **Talk about feelings openly**

Circle time can be used to help students talk about their range of feelings and particularly how we can experience two quite different feelings at the same time.

Consequences

■ **Talking about feelings**

This will revolve mainly around the teacher encouraging students to talk about the feelings they have, about what triggers these feelings and about how these feelings affect their own behaviour and that of others. Describe and praise students' efforts to express verbally how they are feeling. It is important that praise in this instance is given for *talking* about aspects of their emotional experience rather than for simply expressing and managing their emotions appropriately: *'I liked the way you were able to tell us how you were feeling when you found the CD was missing'*.

Teaching personal competences

The following activities can be useful to help students discriminate among their emotions, particularly in individual and small group work.

- **Feelings wheel**

  A 'feelings wheel' can be a fun way to gradually introduce a wider emotion vocabulary. A wheel can be made by photocopying the two circles in **Worksheet 19** on to card, cutting out the two circles, and then fixing them together through the central point. The emotion words written around the outer circumference of the lower circle will be revealed in turn through the aperture cut in the upper circle. The student is asked to suggest, for example, in what circumstance someone might show this emotion. If it is a 'negative' emotion, strategies for managing it and the various ways of expressing it can be discussed. A progressively wider range of emotion words can be developed.

- **Emotions bingo**

  See 'Feelings bingo' on page 96. The student covers the appropriate square with the emotion on it when the stimulus scenario is presented by the adult. The students might also be asked to tell of a time or situation when they or other people have experienced this emotion.

- **Feelings charades**

  Prepare some cards with the names of emotions on them (such as happy, disappointed, proud, sad, afraid, surprised, angry, etc.). A student is asked to pick the top card and then has to act out that feeling. Other students or the adult try to guess what emotion is being portrayed. Similarly, the adult can do the role-play and the student attempts to name the emotion.

- **Talking, Feeling and Doing Game** – see page 52.

- **Mad, Sad, Glad Game** – see page 52.

Finds it difficult to express positive emotions

Some students have predominantly been exposed to the expression of negative, usually angry or anxious emotions. The expression of positive emotions is important to convey worth and value to other people, but it also becomes a prompt and influences the amount of positive emotions we ourselves receive. So students need to learn how to label positive affectionate emotions and also how and when to express them.

Environmental changes

▶ Modelling

The teacher can set the tone of the classroom in general by modelling the expression of positive emotions towards students and by encouraging the use of positive emotions between students. The level of smiling within a classroom is a good litmus test of the emotional literacy levels of that classroom. The teacher can demonstrate positively valuing each individual by, for example, making eye contact and smiling at each student at the beginning and end of each session, and making sure that praise is specific, descriptive and sincere and is accompanied by warmth and openness.

▶ Valuing each other

A concrete way in which teachers can demonstrate the value of students is by a willingness to be at the same level as the students. For example, when talking individually or in small groups, the teacher can sit alongside the students.

▶ Celebrations

The celebration of success, both large and small, in joyful and active ways encourages students to express positive emotions. **Worksheet 6**, 'Celebrate your success', can be photocopied and used in a variety of ways.

▶ Group activities

As a whole class or in a small group, circle time can be used to openly deal with feelings of affection and pride in what other people have done. Videos and artwork can be used to demonstrate how and when we can show positive emotions.

Consequences

■ Welcome positive feelings

Teachers need to be watchful to notice the spontaneous expression of positive emotions between students and to subtly show that they have noticed, approve of and welcome displays of affection and care for each other.

Teaching personal competences

The main problem for students who find it difficult to express positive emotions is either that they do not know how to or because, particularly in males, they think that displays of positive emotions are silly, childish or 'unmanly'. They can learn that this is not the case and can learn the skills needed by being immersed in an ethos in which it is considered fine to display positive emotions. For those who find it very difficult to learn these skills, specific activities like the one below can be undertaken.

● **Role-play positive emotions**

Prepare some cards showing a range of emotions, particularly positive ones. Each card should have a different statement written on it: *'The time I felt …* [happy, pleased, excited, etc.]*'*. Ask individuals in a small group context to role-play how they could communicate each emotion. These role-plays can be captured on video and used again.

● **Expressing positive emotions**

The 'Friendly' and 'Unfriendly' statements activity on page 76 and in **Worksheet 10** is valuable here. It is particularly useful to encourage students to role-play some of the statements.

Many of the other interventions, such as the 'Feelings wheel' (page 98) and 'Feelings charades' (page 98), can also be adapted to support students in expressing positive emotions.

Worksheets

These worksheets may be photocopied for use in your school. Please note that you may enlarge them if needed.

The worksheet required for a particular activity is specified in the notes in the interventions section in the format **Worksheet 1**.

Feelings vocabulary

abandoned	deceitful	glad	lonely	spiritual
abused	defeated	good	loser	strained
accepted	dejected	grateful	loud	stunned
acquiescent	delighted	gratified	lovable	stupid
adamant	dependent	greedy	low	sure
adequate	depressed	grieving	loyal	tempted
affectionate	deprived	groovy	manipulated	tense
affirmed	desperate	guilty	mawkish	threatened
afraid	destructive	gullible	nervous	thwarted
agonised	determined	gutless	nice	tired
alarmed	different	gutted	odd	torn
alienated	diffident	happy	opposed	touched
ambivalent	diminished	hateful	optimistic	touchy
annoyed	disappointed	helpful	outraged	trapped
anxious	discontented	homesick	overlooked	truculent
apathetic	distracted	honoured	overwhelmed	unctuous
appreciated	distraught	hopeful	panicked	upset
astounded	disturbed	hopeless	paranoid	used
attractive	divided	horrible	peaceful	useless
avaricious	dominated	hostile	persecuted	vacuous
averse	dubious	hurt	petrified	violent
awed	eager	hysterical	pleasant	vivacious
awkward	ecstatic	ignored	pleased	vulnerable
bad	elated	immobilised	possessive	wilful
balmy	electrified	impatient	preoccupied	wishy-washy
barmy	embarrassed	imposed upon	pressured	wonderful
beaten	empty	impressed	putrid	worried
beautiful	energetic	inadequate	quarrelsome	zany
bewildered	envious	incompetent	quiet	
bitter	evasive	infatuated	refreshed	
blissful	exasperated	inferior	rejected	
bold	excited	infuriated	relaxed	
bored	exhausted	inhibited	relieved	
brave	exhilarated	insecure	remorseful	
burdened	fabulous	insincere	repulsive	
callous	fantastic	inspired	restless	
caddish	fawning	intimidated	restrained	
cagey	fearful	involved	sad	
cantankerous	flustered	isolated	sapped	
chided	foolish	jaded	satisfied	
churlish	frantic	jealous	scared	
comfortable	free	joyful	screwed up	
concerned	fretful	judgemental	settled	
confident	friendless	jumpy	shallow	
cop out	friendly	kind	shocked	
cowardly	frightened	languid	shy	
creative	frustrated	lazy	silly	
curious	full	left out	sluggish	
cut off	funky	like	sorry	

103

What makes me upset?

Name _____ **Date** _____

- What happened today / yesterday / this week / last week when I became very upset / tearful / angry ... ? (Specify when, where, with whom, etc.)

....

....

....

- What was I thinking to myself while this was happening?

....

....

....

- Was that thought really true / justified? Where is the evidence that supports it?

....

....

....

- There are some people in your class who probably wouldn't get very upset or tearful if the same thing happened to them. What do you think they might be thinking to themselves at that time?

....

....

....

- What might happen to the way you felt about the situation if you were able to think in that way?

....

....

nferNelson
understanding potential

Giving feedback: a teacher–student conversation

Name _____ **Date** _____

- What I liked about your work (or behaviour).

- How I think your work (or behaviour) could be improved.

- How easy or difficult would it be for you to make these improvements in the future?

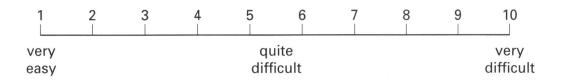

| 1 | 2 | 3 | 4 | 5 | 6 | 7 | 8 | 9 | 10 |

very
easy   quite
difficult   very
difficult

- How could I, or somebody else, help you to be able to make these improvements?

nferNelson
understanding potential

Feelings diary

Name _____ **Date** _____

What I felt today

happy   relaxed   proud   surprised   excited   calm

sad   scared   angry   lonely   frustrated   worried

uncertain   shocked   ← other feelings →

Why I felt that way

What happened?

What thoughts, or pictures, were going through my head when this was happening?

What did I feel?

What did I do because of the way I was feeling?

What happened then? What did other people do because of what I had done?

nferNelson
understanding potential

Feelings graph

Name _____   **Week beginning** _____

Sunday	
Saturday	
Friday	
Thursday	
Wednesday	
Tuesday	
Monday	

Happy   **Neutral**   **Sad**

nferNelson
understanding potential

Celebrate your success

Name _____   **Date** _____

1. Think of all the things you have achieved in your life – all of the things you can do now that you couldn't do before.

2. Write them in the boxes.

Quality log

Name _____   Week beginning _____

Write about any times during the week when you have done something you are proud of.

Monday

Friday

Tuesday

Saturday

Wednesday

Sunday

Thursday

'Well done!'

This worksheet is part of *Emotional Literacy: Assessment and Intervention –
Ages 11 to 16*, ISBN 0-7087-0364-X, and may be photocopied.
Published by nferNelson Publishing Company.
nferNelson is a division of Granada Learning Ltd, part of Granada plc.

nferNelson
understanding potential

What can I do?

Example

You are not allowed to leave the school grounds, but one of your class mates tries to persuade you to go with him down the street to the shops during your lunch break.

What different things can you do?

- Go with him.
- Explain that you do not want to break the school rules, but you would like to go with him after school.
- Tell the teacher what he is doing.
- Tell him off angrily for leaving the school grounds.
- Ring the police.

You took your new calculator to school and it has disappeared from your bag. Another student in your class is using one that looks just like yours.

What different things can you do?

You are playing with some friends and you kick the ball through the window of the house next door. The window smashes.

What different things can you do?

You are in class and everyone is working quietly. You are sharing a book with a partner, but you can't see.

What different things can you do?

You are at school and a group of your class mates are playing football. There is room for one more and you would like to join in.

What different things can you do?

A group of your class mates are walking home together. They refuse to let you accompany them.

What different things can you do?

Your mum comes back from having her hair done. It is cut very short and you don't like it.

What different things can you do?

You promise a friend that you will go to the cinema with her on Saturday, but you are invited to a party that you really want to go to. Your friend is not invited.

What different things can you do?

A new student has just started in your class. You are playing computer games with your friends and the new student is watching you.

What different things can you do?

Your dad won't let you go shopping with your friend until you have tidied up your room.

What different things can you do?

Your teacher is carrying a large pile of books and is having trouble picking up some papers she has dropped.

What different things can you do?

Ways to control angry feelings

Count to 10 slowly **1 2 3 4 5** **6 7 8 9 10**	Take deep breaths 	Traffic lights – STOP! 
Clench fist 3 times 	Draw a picture or write the problem down 	Tell an adult 
Ask to leave the room 	Sit in a quiet place 	Count backwards **10 9 8 7 6** **5 4 3 2 1**

© Southampton City Council 2003.
All rights reserved.
This worksheet is part of *Emotional Literacy: Assessment and Intervention – Ages 11 to 16*, ISBN 0-7087-0364-X, and may be photocopied.
Published by nferNelson Publishing Company.
nferNelson is a division of Granada Learning Ltd, part of Granada plc.

understanding potential

'Friendly' and 'Unfriendly' statement cards

Friendly	Unfriendly
It's okay if other people don't agree with me – not everyone thinks the same way.	I like talking a lot but not listening to everyone else.
I can keep a secret.	I'm always right.
I try to help my friends do their best.	I sometimes tell lies to get others into trouble.
I say nice things to my friends.	I am better than anyone else.
I make people feel happy.	I don't care about other people.
I share things with my friends.	I am better looking than all my friends at school.
I like to be friends with people.	If my friends are wrong, I ignore them.
I never criticise other people.	Sometimes I make my friends cry.
I'm patient.	I argue a lot.
I am honest.	I am the most popular person in class.
I never say anything unkind about other people.	I don't like it when things don't go my way.
I try to make people feel important.	I'm aggressive.
I don't blame other people for things that go wrong.	I tell people what they want to hear, even if it's not true.
I'm a good listener.	I sulk.
If my friends are wrong I try to tell them gently.	I don't like it when other people don't do what I tell them to do.
I like being with other people.	I tease people.
I don't get angry very often.	I am selfish.
I try to help people.	I like to make fun of people.

nferNelson
understanding potential

© Southampton City Council 2003.
All rights reserved.
This worksheet is part of *Emotional Literacy: Assessment and Intervention –*
Ages 11 to 16, ISBN 0-7087-0364-X, and may be photocopied.
Published by nferNelson Publishing Company.
nferNelson is a division of Granada Learning Ltd, part of Granada plc.

Overcoming obstacles

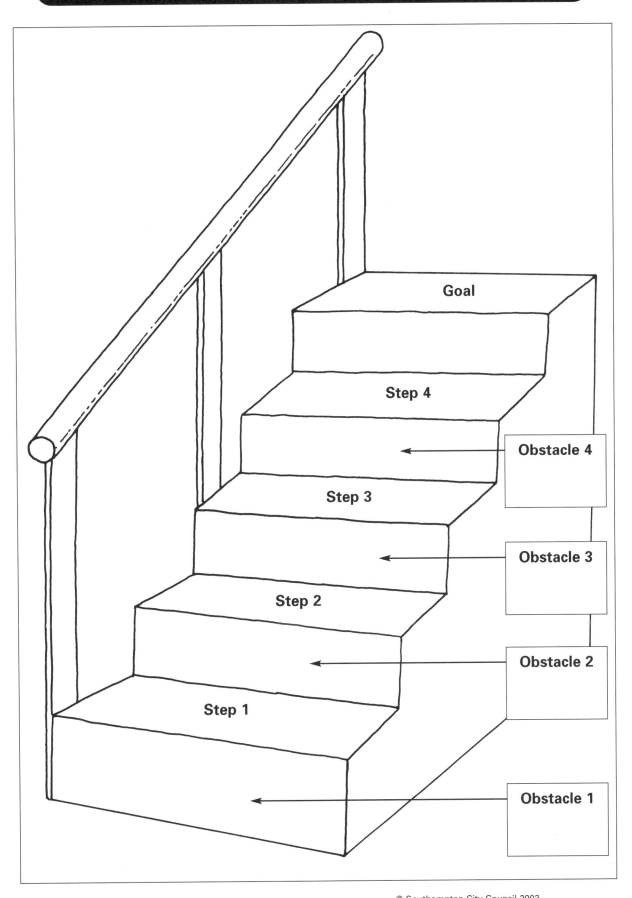

Goal

Step 4

Obstacle 4

Step 3

Obstacle 3

Step 2

Obstacle 2

Step 1

Obstacle 1

This worksheet is part of *Emotional Literacy: Assessment and Intervention –*
Ages 11 to 16, ISBN 0-7087-0364-X, and may be photocopied.
Published by nferNelson Publishing Company.

nferNelson is a division of Granada Learning Ltd, part of Granada plc.

nferNelson
understanding potential

113

Avoiding distractions

Name _____ Date _____

Instructions: Every time you see 3 followed by 2 on the page, circle them.

3 2 1 4 9 6 3 2 3 5

3 4 2 1 3 2 5 9 4 2

1 5 8 4 6 9 3 2 3 2

4 2 3 2 4 6 8 1 5 5

5 6 9 6 2 3 9 7 2 3

8 2 7 5 8 3 4 3 7 1

5 8 3 2 6 2 9 3 5 6

9 6 2 8 6 1 7 3 5 3

5 8 3 2 9 7 5 5 2 8

2 3 5 3 6 8 3 2 5 9

8 5 7 2 5 9 3 6 7 6

7 5 9 3 2 4 6 1 2 3

1 6 9 5 3 2 6 4 8 7

5 3 2 3 2 5 3 2 3 2

Working through a task

Name _____   Date _____

- What do I have to do in this task?

....

....

....

- What parts of this task do I think I will do easily and enjoy?

....

....

....

- What parts do I think I might have difficulty with or not enjoy?

....

....

....

- How difficult will those parts be for me?

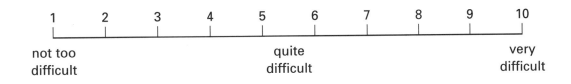

| 1 | 2 | 3 | 4 | 5 | 6 | 7 | 8 | 9 | 10 |

not too
difficult   quite
                                       difficult   very
                                                                              difficult

- How can I reward myself for doing those parts of the work that I might find difficult?

....

....

This worksheet is part of *Emotional Literacy: Assessment and Intervention –
Ages 11 to 16*, ISBN 0-7087-0364-X, and may be photocopied.
Published by nferNelson Publishing Company.

nferNelson
understanding potential

nferNelson is a division of Granada Learning Ltd, part of Granada plc.

Acts of kindness log

Name _____ **Week beginning** _____

It can be fun to do nice things for people as it makes you feel good about yourself as well as making other people feel good.

Try it for one week. Make a pact with yourself that you are going to do one kind thing for someone every day, either at home or at school. Tick the boxes below if you managed to do something kind.

But what sort of things can I do?

Really the list is endless, but here are a few ideas to get you started.

✔ Surprise your parents/carers by tidying up your room without being asked.

✔ Open a door for someone.

✔ Without being asked, do a job around the house – wash up, dust or wash the car.

✔ Say something encouraging to someone who is fed up.

✔ Put some money into a charity collection.

✔ Help your teacher by volunteering to pick up rubbish.

✔ Help a friend with their work at school.

✔ Talk to someone who looks lonely at breaktime.

How was your week?

Did you manage to carry out one kind act every day?

Monday	Tuesday	Wednesday	Thursday	Friday	Saturday	Sunday

nferNelson
understanding potential

When to smile and laugh

Name _____ **Date** _____

1.

Things that make me and other people smile and laugh

e.g. a funny joke

2.

Times when I smile and laugh but I don't feel happy

e.g. when a teacher reprimands me, sometimes I smile so other people don't know I'm upset

3.

Things that make me smile or laugh but might upset other people

e.g. you may smirk or laugh when someone trips up

This worksheet is part of *Emotional Literacy: Assessment and Intervention – Ages 11 to 16*, ISBN 0-7087-0364-X, and may be photocopied.
Published by nferNelson Publishing Company.
nferNelson is a division of Granada Learning Ltd, part of Granada plc.

nferNelson
understanding potential

Sort and match cards

Examples of situation cards	Examples of response cards
I am stuck with my work.	Say to an adult: 'Please can you help me.'
I need to talk to the first-aider during class.	Talk to a friend.
A stranger wants me to get into a car.	Talk to an adult quietly about what you need.
I've had an argument with my friend.	Shout or scream.
My parents keep having arguments.	Run away.
Someone has taken something from my bag.	Talk to someone at home.
People are picking on me and teasing me.	Talk to a teacher.

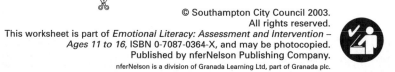

nferNelson
understanding potential

© Southampton City Council 2003.
All rights reserved.
This worksheet is part of *Emotional Literacy: Assessment and Intervention –*
Ages 11 to 16, ISBN 0-7087-0364-X, and may be photocopied.
Published by nferNelson Publishing Company.
nferNelson is a division of Granada Learning Ltd, part of Granada plc.

Feelings bingo

angry	happy		thoughtful
scared		bored	excited
	proud	bad tempered	sad
angry	sad	happy	
scared	aggressive		excited
	proud	lonely	embarrassed

nferNelson
understanding potential

Feelings bingo

mad		angry	pleased
cheerful	afraid		proud
sad		happy	upset
shocked	glad		sad
cross	angry	jolly	
proud		happy	gloomy

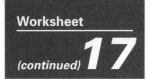

nferNelson
understanding potential

Feelings bingo

angry	sad	happy	thoughtful
scared	aggressive	bored	excited
satisfied	proud	lonely	embarrassed
jolly	jumpy	mad	bad tempered
unhappy	gloomy	frightened	cheerful
wonderful	fed up	snappy	shocked
surprised	upset	afraid	cross
glad	hurt	ashamed	pleased

nferNelson

understanding potential

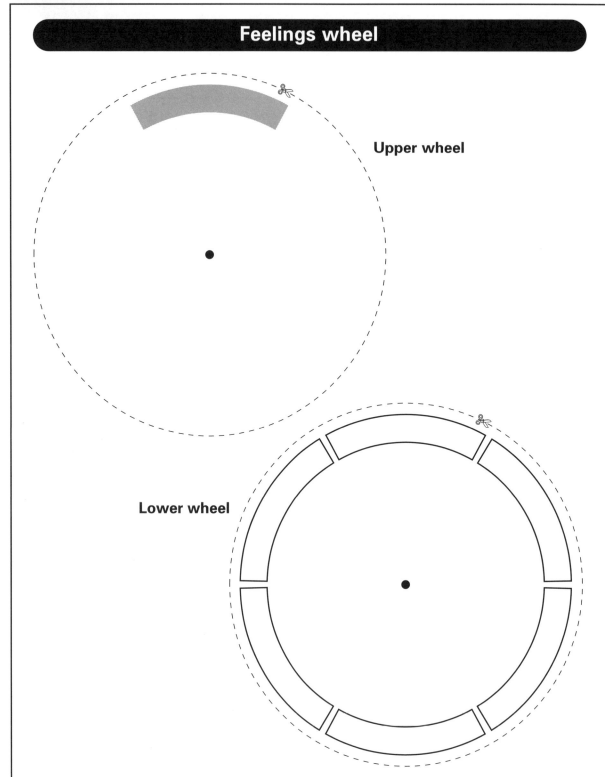

Feelings wheel

Upper wheel

Lower wheel

1. Photocopy on to card, enlarging as desired.

2. Write emotion words of your choice on the lower wheel.

3. Cut out the shaded part of the upper wheel to make an aperture.

4. Fix the upper wheel over the lower wheel at the centre point so that it can still turn freely.

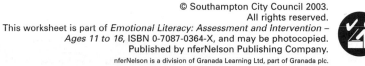

Emotional Literacy Checklists

 The checklists and the Student Score Sheet may be photocopied for use in your school. You may delete the page numbers if you feel they might distract the respondents.

Emotional Literacy Student Checklist

Ages 11 to 16

First name .... **Surname** ....

Date .... **Year group** ☐ **Male** ○ **Female** ○

Here are some questions about you. Please try to answer them as honestly as you can. Read each question and then put a tick in one of the boxes. Make sure you do each question.

Here is an example of how to answer the questions. If you do not think you are good at many things, you would tick the box 'not like me at all'.

	Very like me	Quite like me	Only a bit like me	Not like me at all
I am good at many things.				✔

Now please answer the rest of the questions.

		Very like me	Quite like me	Only a bit like me	Not like me at all
1	I try to listen to other people's views even when I think they are wrong.				
2	I often forget what I should be doing.				
3	I am aware of my own strengths and weaknesses.				
4	I often lose my temper.				
5	A lot of people seem to like me.				
6	I know when people are starting to get upset.				
7	I tend to leave things to the last minute.				
8	When I'm sad, I usually know the reason why.				
9	I get upset if I do badly at something.				
10	I can make new friends easily.				
11	I get annoyed when other people get things wrong.				

Please turn over

© Southampton City Council 2003.
All rights reserved.
This checklist is part of *Emotional Literacy: Assessment and Intervention –
Ages 11 to 16*, ISBN 0-7087-0364-X, and may be photocopied.
Published by nferNelson Publishing Company.
nferNelson is a division of Granada Learning Ltd, part of Granada plc.

nferNelson
understanding potential

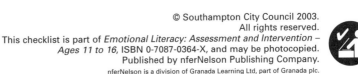

125 ●

		Very like me	Quite like me	Only a bit like me	Not like me at all
12	I carry on trying even if I find the work difficult.				
13	I am easily hurt by what others say about me.				
14	I calm down quickly after I have got upset.				
15	I am rather a shy person.				
16	When I notice people getting upset, I try to help them feel better.				
17	I make a good effort with most of my school work.				
18	I tend to put myself down even when I have done something well.				
19	I am usually a calm person.				
20	I spend too much time alone.				
21	I try to help someone who is being bullied.				
22	I get distracted easily from what I'm supposed to be doing.				
23	I worry a lot about the things I'm not good at.				
24	I can wait patiently for my turn.				
25	I can make friends again after a row.				

Thank you for filling in this checklist.

nferNelson
understanding potential

Emotional Literacy Teacher Checklist

Ages 11 to 16

Student's name .... **Completed by** ....

Date .... **Year group** ☐ **Male** ◯ **Female** ◯

Please look at each statement and put a tick in the box that best describes how this student generally is. There are no right or wrong answers. Please ensure you answer all the questions.

	Very true	Somewhat true	Not really true	Not at all true
1 Listens to other people's point of view in a discussion or argument.				
2 Gives up easily when faced with something difficult.				
3 Is aware of his/her own strengths and qualities.				
4 Loses temper when loses at a game or in a competition.				
5 Laughs and smiles when it is appropriate to do so.				
6 Is intolerant of people who are different from him/her.				
7 When starts a task or assignment, usually follows it through to completion.				
8 Finds it hard to accept constructive criticism and feedback.				
9 Is liable to sulk if doesn't get his/her own way.				
10 Makes the right kind of eye contact when interacting with others.				
11 Is insensitive to the feelings of others.				
12 Leaves things to the last minute.				
13 Can recognise the early signs of becoming angry.				
14 Remains calm and composed when loses or 'fails' at something.				
15 Is disliked by many of his/her peers.				
16 Is very critical of others' shortcomings.				
17 Does things when they need to be done.				
18 Can name or label his/her feelings.				
19 When things go wrong, immediately denies that it is his/her fault or blames others.				
20 Has a sense of humour and fun that is used appropriately.				

© Southampton City Council 2003.
All rights reserved.
This checklist is part of *Emotional Literacy: Assessment and Intervention –
Ages 11 to 16*, ISBN 0-7087-0364-X, and may be photocopied.
Published by nferNelson Publishing Company.
nferNelson is a division of Granada Learning Ltd, part of Granada plc.

nferNelson
understanding potential

127 ●

Emotional Literacy Parent Checklist

Ages 11 to 16

We would be very grateful if you could complete the attached checklist for your child.

What is this checklist about?

This checklist is part of a set of materials designed to assess the emotional literacy of young people. It asks for the views of parents or primary carers on the emotional literacy of their child. The purpose of the checklist is to discover where young people's strengths are in this area. Should your child be experiencing any difficulties, the result will also help us know how best to support your child.

What is emotional literacy?

Emotional literacy concerns the ability of people to recognise, understand, handle and appropriately express their own emotions, and to recognise, understand and respond appropriately to the expressed emotions of others.

Through looking at emotional literacy, schools are encouraged to focus on important aspects of behaviour and learning, such as the emotions, as well as academic achievement.

How to complete the checklist

There are 25 statements about your child. Any parent or primary carer of the child may answer them, but please answer the questions in the way in which you *personally* see your child. For each statement, put a tick in the box that best describes your child – there are no right or wrong answers.

Confidentiality

Any information you give will be treated in accordance with the Data Protection Act. It will be treated in strictest confidence by the school.

What to do with the completed checklist

Once you have completed the checklist, please return it to the school. Thank you.

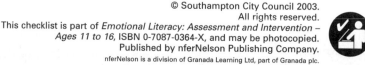

nferNelson
understanding potential

Emotional Literacy Parent Checklist

Ages 11 to 16

Child's name .... Date ....

School .... Year group ☐   Male ○   Female ○

Please look at each statement and put a tick in the box that best describes how you think your child generally is. There are no right or wrong answers. Please make sure you answer each question. Your responses will be treated in strictest confidence.

		Very true	Somewhat true	Not really true	Not at all true
1	Listens to other people's point of view in a discussion or argument.				
2	Gives up easily when things aren't perfect.				
3	Can name or label his/her feelings.				
4	Is quick tempered and aggressive.				
5	Spends too much time alone.				
6	Is tolerant of people who are different from him/her.				
7	Seems able to shut out distractions when needs to focus.				
8	Tends to have feelings of self-doubt/insecurity.				
9	Is liable to sulk if doesn't get his/her own way.				
10	Finds it difficult to make new friends.				
11	Is insensitive to the feelings of others.				
12	When starts a task, usually follows it through to completion.				
13	Can recognise the early signs of becoming angry.				
14	When things go wrong, immediately denies that it is his/her fault or blames others.				
15	Is liked by a lot of people.				
16	Is very critical of others' shortcomings.				
17	Leaves things to the last minute.				
18	Is aware of his/her own strengths and weaknesses.				
19	Rushes into things without really thinking.				
20	Can make friends again after a row.				
21	Gets annoyed when other people get things wrong.				
22	Keeps trying even when faced with something difficult.				
23	Is easily hurt by what others say about him/her.				
24	Is a bad loser.				
25	Mixes with other children.				

Thank you for completing this checklist. Please return the completed checklist to the school.

nferNelson
understanding potential

© Southampton City Council 2003.
All rights reserved.
This checklist is part of *Emotional Literacy: Assessment and Intervention –
Ages 11 to 16*, ISBN 0-7087-0364-X, and may be photocopied.
Published by nferNelson Publishing Company.
nferNelson is a division of Granada Learning Ltd, part of Granada plc.

Student Score Sheet

Student's name .... **Completed by** ....

Date .... **Year group** ☐ **Male** ◯ **Female** ◯

	Overall emotional literacy score	Self-awareness subscale score	Self-regulation subscale score	Motivation subscale score	Empathy subscale score	Social skills subscale score
Student Checklist						
Teacher Checklist						
Parent Checklist						

Profile of subscale scores from the Teacher Checklist

Subscale scores on Teacher Checklist

Self-awareness · Self-regulation · Motivation · Empathy · Social skills

Profile of subscale scores from the Parent Checklist

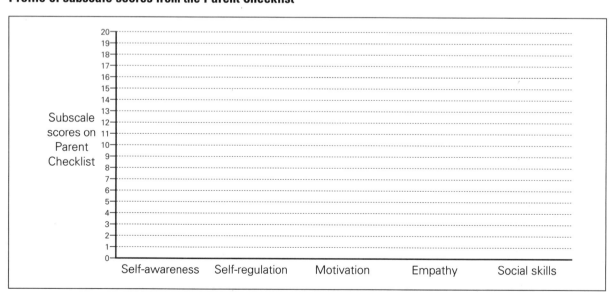

Subscale scores on Parent Checklist

Self-awareness · Self-regulation · Motivation · Empathy · Social skills

nferNelson
understanding potential